AF621904

Carrying Enemies on Your Shoulder : Indian Folk Wisdom in Tibet

Bibliotheca Indo-Buddhica Series
SUNIL GUPTA, Editor

Bibliotheca Indo Buddhica Series No. 166

Carrying Enemies on Your Shoulder : Indian Folk Wisdom in Tibet

Hugh Meredith Flick, Jr.

Sri Satguru Publications
A Division of
Indian Books Centre
Delhi - 110007

Published by:
Sri Satguru Publications
Indological and Oriental Publishers
A Division of
Indian Books Centre
40/5, Shakti Nagar,
Delhi-110007
(INDIA)

All Rights Reserved

First Edition: Delhi, 1996

ISBN 81-7030-479-2

No part of this book may be used or reproduced in any manner whatsoever without written permission except in the case of brief quotations embodied in critical articles and reviews.

Printed at
D.K. Fine Art Press (P) Ltd.
Delhi 110 052
Printed in India.

Preface

This study of the *Nītiśāstra* of Masūrākṣa was begun several years ago as a means of examining one aspect of folklore in India. *Nīti* verses are an important part of the heritage of folklore from ancient India. Although the focus of this study is on a single collection of *nīti* verses, the processes involved in its compilation and proliferation illustrate the dynamics of the interrelation between folklore and written literature. This particular collection is also significant since it provides a case study of the cultural interaction between India and Tibet. This study is only the beginning of a more comprehensive inquiry into the nature of the oral tradition in ancient India.

The library facilities at Harvard contain three of the four available recensions of the *bsTan 'Gyur*. The *sDe-dGe* Edition and the *sNar-Thang* Edition in wood-block printed bundles are housed in the Harvard-Yenching Library. The *Cone* Edition is available on microfiche in the Harvard-Yenching Library as well. The *Peking* Edition is available on interlibrary loan from the University of Indiana Library. The Sanskrit collection in Widener Library, Harvard University, contains all the major references used in the process individual verses in various Sanskrit works.

I wish to express my sincere gratitude to Professor Daniel H.H. Ingalls for his guidance throughout my work with *nīti* verses. Under his direction I have been able to read widely within Sanskrit narrative literature. This has been especially useful for my work as an Instructor in Folklore and Mythology. Professor Ingalls suggested many useful references and sources for the particular verses in Masūrākṣa's collection. He also provided me with many useful suggestions on Sanskrit verses.

I would like to thank Professor Masatoshi Nagatomi for the long hours he spent helping me iron out the subtleties of certain of the Tibetan verses and helping me make sense out of others. Professor Nagatomi also made many valuable suggestions concerning my research on the cultural interaction between India and Tibet. I would also like to thank Mr. Siddiq Wahid and the Venerable Tulku Thondup who helped me with their personal knowledge of colloquial and classical Tibetan.

I wish to extend my very special thanks to Harriet Caplan, whose patience and support lasted through the numerous drafts of this dissertation. Her encouragement and moral support were instrumental.

Contents

List of Charts

Abbreviations

Cr	Sternbach, Ludwik, ed. *Cāṇakya-Nīti-Text Tradition*. Vol. II, Parts I-III. Hoshiarpur: Vishveshvaranand Vedic Research Institute, 1967-70.
CL	Sternbach. *Cāṇakya* Vol. I, Part II. (Laghu-Cāṇakya Version)
CN	Sternbach. *Cāṇakya* Vol. I, Part I. (Cāṇakya-Nīti-Śāstra Version)
CR	Sternbach. *Cāṇakya* Vol. I, Part II. (Cāṇakya-Rāja-Nīti-Śāstra Version)
CS	Sternbach. *Cāṇakya* Vol. I. (Cāṇakya-Sāra-Saṃgraha Version)
CV	Sternbach. *Cāṇakya* Vol. I, Part I. (Vṛddha-Cāṇakya-Ornatior Version)
Cv	Sternbach. *Cāṇakya* Vol. I, Part I. (Vṛddha-Cāṇakya-Simplicior Version)
GP	Bhattacharya, R., ed. *Garuḍapurāṇam of Maharsi Vedavyāsa*. Varanasi : Chaukhambha Sanskrit Sansthan, 1964.
HH	*The Hitopadeśa in the Sanskrita Language*. London : Library, East-India House, 1810.
HJ	Johnson, F., ed. *Hitopadeśa. The Sanskrit Text With a Grammatical Analysis Alphabetically Arranged*. London : W.H. Allen and Co., 1847.
HK	Kale, M.R., ed. *The Hitopadiśa of Nāryāna*. Bombay : Oriental Publishing Company, 1915.
HM	Muller, M., ed. *The First Book of the Hitopadeśa*. London : Longman, Green, Longman, Roberts, and Green, 1964. *The Second, Third, and Fourth Books of the Hitopadeśa*. London : Longman, Green, Longman, Roberts, and Green, 1865.
HP	Peterson, P., ed. *Hitopadeśa by Nārāyana*. Bombay : Government Central Book Depot, 1887.
HS	Schlegel, A.G. and Lassen, C., eds. *Hitopadeśas id est Institutio Salutaris*. Bonnae ad Rhenum : Eduardum Weber, 1829.
IS	Bohtlingk, O., ed. *Indische Spruche*. St. Petersberg : Eggers et co., 1870-73.

MBh Sukthankar, V.S., ed. *The Mahābhārata-Critical Edition.* Poona: Bhandarkar Oriental Research Institute, 1933-59.

MSS Sternbach, L., ed. *The Mahāsubhāṣita-Samgraha* Hoshiarpur : Vishveshvaranand Vedic Research Institute, 1974

PKB Kielhorn, F. and Buhler, G., eds. *Pañcatantra* I-V. Bombay : Government Central Book Depot, 1879-81.

PP Hertel, J., ed. *The Pañcatantra.* Cambridge : Harvard University Press, 1908, 1912.

PRE Edgerton, F., ed. *The Pañcatantra Reconstructed.* New Haven: American Oriental Society, 1924.

PS Hertel, J., ed. *Das sudliche Pañcatantra.* Leipzig : B.G. Teubner, 1906.

PT Hertel, J., ed. *Uber das Tantrākhyāyika, die Kaśmīrische Rezension des Pancatantra.* Leipzig : B.G. Teubner, 1904.

PTK Hertel, J., ed. *The Pañcatantra.* Cambridge : Harvard University Press, 1915.

SP Peterson, P., ed. *The Paddhati of Sārṅgadhara.* Bombay : Government Central Book, Depot, 1888.

SRBh Paraba, K.P., ed. *Subhāsita-Ratna-Bhāṇḍāgāra.* Bombay : Nirnayasagara Press, 1886.

SRK Bhatavadekar, K.S., ed. *Subhāṣitaratnākara.* Bombay : Gopal Narayen and Col, 1888.

SS Krishnamoorthy, K., ed. *Sāyana's Subhāṣita-Sudhānidhi.* Dharwar : Karnatak University, 1968..

SV Peterson, P., ed. *The Subhāsitāvali of Vallabhadeva.* Bombay: Education Society's Press, 1886.

1

The tapestry of the cultural interaction between Indian and Tibet is an intricate interweaving of many patterns and threads. Although India and Tibet are geographically contiguous there has not been a continuous tradition of cultural interaction. The impenetrability of the Himālayas served to isolate Tibet from its neighbor to the south for long stretches of time. Even during these periods of relative isolation there was undoubtedly some cultural exchange as wanderers and traders from one culture mixed with those of the other, exchanging ideas and stories as well as goods and services. However, it is clear that large scale cultural contact did not take place during these periods. Although the most evident cultural interaction between Tibet and Indian involved religion, there were many other interactions as well. Many of these interactions involved areas of human activity normally associated with folklore. Included in these inter-changes were folk customs, folk arts, folk songs, folk narratives, material folk culture, and folk wisdom. The oral traditions of each culture, being the repositories of much of this material, absorbed and assimilated the exchanged material. The best method for studying such exchanges would be extensive field work throughout both countries over a period of time. However, since such studies have not been conducted and are not available for research, the next best indicators available for research are written sources of various kinds. These written sources include transcriptions from the oral traditions of each individual culture as well as original compositions by literate authors and translations of written sources from the other culture.

One of the generic groups of folklore which crosses cultural boundaries very readily is folk wisdom. Since folk wisdom is an important part of an active oral tradition it is often preserved in the form of short verses. Such verses may become stylized but are still subject to the dynamic processes of the oral tradition so that there can be no fixed authoritative form of any such verse. Very little of such folk wisdom from the Tibetan oral tradition has survived in written sources but a substantial amount has been preserved in various forms from the Indian oral tradition.

A common feature of ancient Indian oral traditional narrative was the short sententious verses which were sprinkled throughout the prose narratives as well as the poetic narratives.

> Most of the works of Sanskrit literature contain a countless number of moral and ethical verses. These verses that are preserved in metrical form are mines of practical good sense.[1]

> Their content is the bedrock of common sense and prejudice, but they show a sophisticated literary style which makes use of parallelism, chiasmus, balanced grammatical structure, and metre.[2]

> They are drawn from real life and give the fruit of philosophy grafted on the stem of experience; they furnish an index to the spirit of a nation and are a result of its civilization.[3]

These verses are constructed and used in the same way that two-line formulaic expressions and short verbatim passages are constructed and used in the Serbo-Croatian oral tradition according to the work done by A.B. Lord.[4]

> In India most of these wise sayings in poetical form, mostly composed in *śloka*-s or *anuṣṭubh*-s belonged to the mass of oral tradition; they were not assembled in any collections but floated freely.[5]

> In content many of them are comparable to the proverbs of folklore, while in style they are more like the 'proverbs' of solomon.[6]

These proverbial and moral verses were undoubtedly based on non-poetic proverbial expressions that had their origins at the most grass roots levels. The process of formulating folk wisdom in proverbs is common to cultures throughout the world. It was the wisdom and common sense embodied in these simple proverbs that one generation would pass on to the next generation. The popularity of the narrative helped proliferate these couplets and their inherent practicality caused them to be remembered and recited on fitting occasions. The process in which these simple folk proverbs became molded into the polished verses which are found in so many Sanskrit texts may very well have been carried out mostly by the poets of the oral tradition of ancient India. Their training and expertise in the use of the main narrative metres, *śloka* and *anuṣṭubh*, would have enabled them to take the simple prose expressions and recast them in perfect metrical form. Within an oral tradition such as the Serbo-Croation oral tradition the composition of highly polished verses is very common.[7] Each oral traditional poet may have had his own version of any particular common expression that he made use of in his performances. The very nature of the oral traditional process also left him free to make use of any better formulation that he happened to hear himself directly or indirectly from other poets or singers. These sententious verses could then be used in any number of different narrative situations as the poet needed them to emphasize some bit of wisdom or teach an important lesson. When these verses are considered to be part of an oral tradition they take on added significance in terms of cultural importance since only the most meaningful material is transmitted from generation to generation in an oral tradition. In addition, any question as to their association with any particular author becomes meaningless within an oral tradition.

These sententious and didactic verses were traditionally considered to belong to three different sciences, or *śāstras*, by the Indians. They were divided according to the subject matter with which they dealt into these three *śāstras: dharma, artha*, and *nīti. Dharma* verses dealt primarily with moral issues and were related to legal precedents.

> *Dharma* (from the root *dhṛ-* 'to hold') comprehends acts which a person is under any duty of fulfill (iti-kartavyatā), provided that it has a moral, social, or superstitious significance, and does not arise from mere convenience.[8]
>
> *Dharma* texts...deal after all with duty and morality as the basis for law.[9]

Artha verses and *nīti* verses were closely connected and were often indistinguishable. Basically, however, *artha* verses deal with ways to create benefit for oneself particularly at the royal level of the social hierarchy.

> The Arthaśāstra is concerned with profit, and it is not concerned with religion or duty save insofar as it can use the former to advance the interest of the prince, or the latter is good policy to win popular affection, for instance, in a conquered state.[10]

Nīti verses can also refer to ways of succeeding in the world even on the royal level but in general *nīti* verses contain expressions of common sense and prejudice. In regard to *nīti* verses that are concerned with royal matters:

> This royal advice never becomes elaborate nor technical as it is in the *Arthaśāstra*, but the similarity of the subject matter may have been enough to attribute the proverbs to the reputed author of the *Arthaśāstra*.[11]

There is a great deal of overlap among these three types of sententious verse, especially between the *Arthaśāstra* and the *Nītiśāstra*. Of these three types of verses, *nīti* verses and *artha* verses are more often associated with oral traditional narrative although *dharma* verses were also sometimes found in oral traditional material.

> The fable, indeed, is essentially connected with the two branches of science known by the Indians as the *Nītiśāstra* and the *Arthaśāstra*, which have this in common as opposed to the *Dharmaśāstra* that they are not codes of morals, but deal with man's action in practical politics and conduct of the ordinary affairs of everyday life and intercourse.[12]

It is not clear at what point collections of these verses began to be put together into compendia but a great many of these verses were preserved nowhere else. These *Subhāṣita-Saṃgrahas* were sometimes devoted to a single subject, to a single type of verse, or could be almost random collections of verses including verses on love, nature, etc. In some of these *saṃgrahas* the verses are ascribed to various authors and appear to have been culled from longer texts, many of which are no longer available. *Nīti* verses were the popular subject of many of these collections.

> The most famous and well-known *subhāṣitas* containing sententious sayings, which belonged to the floating mass of oral tradition, were probably strung together in the beginning of the Christian era; then they were also attributed to a well-known author in *majorem gloriam*. Probably Bhartṛhari's epigrams and Cāṇakya's sayings became thus known.[13]

Cāṇakya's name became associated with all types of sententious verse and many different collections of such verses which probably came straight out of the oral tradition were ascribed to him. This undoubtedly served to authenticate and legitimize the particular collection in the same way the name of Vyāsa became connected to the arrangement of the Vedas as well as to the composition of the *Mahābhārata* and, in Greece, Homer's name became associated with not only the Homeric epics but also the Homeric Hymns. Although most of the Cāṇakya verses are *nīti* verses, they also deal with other types of subject matter.

> Thus the Cāṇakya collections contain examples of three great types of Sanskrit literature: the proverbial literature of *nīti*, the pedagogical literature of *dharma*, and the courtly literature of love and honor.[14]

> Among the most popular secular works of Sanskrit literature are the collections of verse maxims attributed to Cāṇakya...Cāṇakya verses have been borrowed from other collections and have been borrowed into other collections, so that there is not a general Sanskrit anthology of the past thousand years that entirely lacks them.[15]

Ludwik Sternbach, as a result of editing various texts and manuscripts of Cāṇakya's verses, decided that "all the known Cāṇakya's compendia can be divided into no more than six versions.[16] D.H.H. Ingalls has shown that Sternbach's conclusions were not based on a comprehensive enough examination of the textual and especially the manuscript evidence.[17] In addition, if one considers that the bulk of the *nīti* verses were once part of an oral tradition, then it is highly unlikely that there would be any fixed number of the ways in which these would be collected. Many of the extant texts and manuscripts are undoubtedly scions of collections made many centuries ago, but to limit this number is naive.

Cāṇakya's name is not the only one associated with *nīti* verses, but it certainly is the main one. In the *Garuḍa Purāṇa*, a whole *nītiśāstra*, which is almost identical to many of what Sternbach labels "Cāṇakya Rājanīti Śāstras," is ascribed to Bṛhaspati.[18] In the *Mahābhārata*, Vidura is credited with a great many wise sayings in the form of common *nīti* verses.[19] Also in the *Mahābhārata*, Bhīṣma, in the *Śanti Parva*, mentions a whole series of *nīti* verses which he ascribes to the *ṛshi* Bharadvāja.[20] The name of Bhartṛhari is also associated with *nīti* verses. It seems likely that many personal collections of favorite verses were made by individual scholars throughout the centuries and committed to manuscript. However, because of the problems of preservation of manuscripts in India any manuscripts would have had to have been recopied periodically or they would have been lost. This need for regular reproduction served as a natural selection process with only the fittest manuscripts able to survive. Many individual verses from these personal collections were in turn collected into other *saṃgrahas* such as Vallabhadeva's *Subhāṣitāvali*.[22] Many of the collections that were recopied lost their association with an individual collator and joined the large mass of collections ascribed to one of the general "authorities" such as Cāṇakya.

One example of a collection of *nīti* verses that is not ascribed to Cāṇakya is the *Nītiśāstra* of Masūrākṣa. Unfortunately the Sanskrit original has not survived, but a translation of it in Tibetan is found in the Tibetan *bsTan 'Gyur*.[23] Many of the verses in this *nītiśāstra* are standard ones found in various Cāṇakya manuscripts and texts and some do not seem to appear anywhere else. It seems most likely that Masūrākṣa drew both from manuscript sources and from oral traditional sources to put together this particular *nītiśāstra*. In the first verse of the collection, Masūrākṣa states that he collected the verses from various *śāstras* of *artha* (*don gyi bstan dcos bye brag las.*)[24] This manuscript seems somewhat typical of a general collecting activity on the part of various teachers and scholars who gathered together the verses that they liked best or which were the best for instructional purposes out of the mass of oral traditional verses or from other manuscripts. These manuscripts would probably often become labeled as Cāṇakya collections because of the association of Cāṇakya's name with the *nīti* verses of the oral tradition. Ones that were not identified with Cāṇakya were probably soon lost since they would not be recopied as the manuscripts deteriorated or when they were recopied, they would be authenticated and legitimized by association with the master of all *nīti* verses, Cāṇakya.

The *Nītiśāstra* of Masūrākṣa is interesting and worthy of special consideration for many reasons. As an example of ninth century collections of *nīti* verses, Masūrākṣa's collection is an indicator of the range of verses that were popular during that period. By examining the narrative literature and the collections of verses which are thought by scholars to have been composed around the ninth century or prior to this period, it is possible to see the sources that Masūrākṣa may have used and, to some extent, the popular sources of the period. By examining the variants of these as they appear in the possible sources as well as those that appear in later collections, a strong case can be made for the connection of these verses with an active oral tradition. In such an oral tradition the texts would not be arbitrarily fixed but would be subject to variation according to the creativity and imagination of the various poets who made use of the basic concept expressed in the verse.

Masūrākṣa's text is also interesting because it represents a point of cultural interaction between India and Tibet. It was chosen by the Tibetan compilers of the *bsTan 'Gyur* as a piece of secular Indian literature worth translating and preserving in their sacred writings. By examining the evidence concerning the date of its translation into Tibetan and the identity of its translators, the process of this type of cultural interaction can be studied. Although the *Nītiśāstra* of Masūrākṣa represents only a small thread within the whole tapestry of cultural interaction between India and Tibet, it is worthy of careful examination since it is out of such threads that the whole tapestry is woven.

Notes

1. L. Sternbach, *Subhāṣita, Gnomic, and Didactic Literature* (Wiesbaden: Otto Harrassowitz, 1974), P. 1.
2. D.H.H. Ingalls, "The Cāṇakya Collections and Nārāyaṇa's Hitopadeśa," *Journal of the American Oriental Society* 96 (1966), p. 1.
3. Sternbach, *Subhāṣita*, p. 1.
4. A.B. Lord, *The Singer of Tales* (New York: Atheneum, 1976).
5. Sternbach, *Subhāṣita*, p. 1.
6. Ingalls, "the Cāṇakya Collections," p. 1.
7. Lord, *The Singer of Tales*.
8. J.D.M. Derritt, *Dharma Śāstra and Judicial Literature* (Weisbaden: Otto Harrassowitz, 1974), p. 4.
9. A.B. Keith, *A History of Sanskrit Literature* (Oxford: Clarendon Press, 1928), p. 451.
10. *Ibid.*, p. 451.
11. Ingalls, "The Cāṇakya Collections," p. 2.
12. Keith, *History*, p. 243
13. Sternbach, *Subhāṣita*, p. 4.
14. Ingalls, "The Cāṇakya Collections," p. 4.
15. *Ibid.*, p. 1.
16. Ludwik Sternbach, *Cāṇakya-Nīti-Text Tradition* Vol. 1., Part 1 (Hoshiarpur: Visveshvaranand Vedic Research Institute, 1963), p. ix.
17. Ingalls, "The Cāṇakya Collections," p. 8.
18. R. Bhattacharya (Editor), *Garuḍapurāṇam* (Varanasi: Chaukhambha Sanskrit Sansthan, 1964).
19. V.S. Sukthankar (Ed.). *The Mahābhārat-Critical Edition* (Poona: Bhandarkar Oriental Research Institute, 1933-59). Vidura makes use of *nīti* wisdom on many occasions. *Mahābhārata* 5.35. -5.40 contains a whole discourse on *nīti* made by Vidura.
20. The *Mahābhārata* 12. 138.
21. M.R. Kale, *The Nīti and Vāirāgya Śatakas of Bhartṛhari* (Delhi: Motilal Banarsidass, 1971). Bhartṛhari's verses do not appear in any cāṇakya collections. Bhartṛhari seems to have written them himself or taken them from a branch of the oral tradition which was never recorded elsewhere.

22. P. Peterson, *The Subhāṣitāvali of Vallabhadeva* (Bombay: Education Society's Press, 1886). Vallabhadeva cites the sources for many of his verses. Some of these references are the only mention of the particular author or compiler.
23. The *Nītiśāstra* of Masūrākṣa appears in all four recensions of the *bsTan-' Gyur* available. These are the *sDe dge Edition*; the *sNar Thang Edition*; the *Cone Edition*, and the *Peking Edition*.
24. *The nītiśāstra of Masūrākṣa* verse 1.1.

2

Very little is known about the compilation and proliferation of the *Nītiśāstra* of Masūrākṣa. The Sanskrit original has not survived. The work is preserved only in a Tibetan translation, which is included in the *bsTan 'Gyur*. The information concerning its author and date is modest. Masūrākṣa's *Nītiśāstra* forms only a small segment of the cultural interaction between India and Tibet but it can serve as a representative case study of the process as a whole. The social and religious forces which prompted its composition and its introduction into Tibet are the same ones which brought about the multifaceted cultural interaction between India and Tibet.

In the opening verse of the *Nītiśāstra* in question we have reference to someone named Masūrākṣa as the compiler of the *Nītiśāstra*:

> don gyi bstan bcos bye brag las
> bstan bcos bdag la phan pa daṅ
> mi rnams blo ni bskyed bya'i phyir
> ma su ra kshas bsdus te bshad[1]

> Having collected verses from various *śāstras* of *artha*,
> Masūrākṣa has related this *śāstra* for our benefit and
> for the sake of producing intelligence in men.

At the end of each section in the *sDe-dGe* and the *Cone* editions of the *Nītiśāstra* there is the mention of Masūrākṣa's name again.

> ma su ra khas byas pa'i lugs kyi bstan bcos las le'u dan pao.[2]

> Thus ends the first section of the *Nītiśāstra* written by Masūrākṣa.

Unfortunately there are very few reference in Sanskrit literature to anyone by the name of Masūrākṣa. Only two references were found in Sanskrit literature which mention the name Masūrākṣa. The most useful reference is found in Vallabhadeva's fifteenth century *subhāṣita-saṃgraha*, the *Subhāṣitāvali*.[3] Masūrākṣa is also mentioned in one of the *gātha* verses of the *Laṅkāvatāra Sūtra*.[4]

Vallabhadeva attributes many of the 3527 verses he included in the *subhāṣitāvali* to individual authors. He attributes verse 2935 to Masūrākṣa.

> yad apasarati mesaḥ kāraṇaṃ tat prahartuṃ
> mṛgapatir atikopāt saṃkucaty utpatiṣṇuḥ
> hṛdayanihitavāira gūdḥamantropacārāḥ
> kimiva hi gaṇayanto buddhimantaḥ kṣamante
> Masāurākṣasya.[5]

In the Tibetan translation this is verse number 3.16. The fact that Vallabhadeva makes reference to Masūrākṣa by name is a good indication that he had access to a copy of Masūrākṣa's *Nītiśāstra* or to some other lost manuscript that quoted Masūrākṣa by name. Vallabhadeva also includes ten other verses which are also found in Masūrākṣa's work but none of these verses has a reference to an individual's name.[6] In fact, the verse which Vallabhadeva attributes to Masūrākṣa also appears in several recensions of the *Pañcatantra*.[7] Masūrākṣa's source for this verse was undoubtedly the *Pañcatantra* and Vallabhadeva either overlooked the fact that this was a verse from the *Pañcatantra* or had a recension of the *Pañcatantra* which did not contain this verse.

Another mention of someone named Masūrākṣa appears in the *Laṅkāvatāra Sūtra*. Masūrākṣa is included in a quarter of great *ṛṣi*-s who will appear sometime in the future.

> Valmīko masurākṣas ca kāutilya aśvalāyanaḥ.
> ṛsayaś ca mahābhāga bhaviṣyanti anāgate.[8]

The date of composition of the *Laṅkāvatāra Sūtra* is not certain.

> The one thing that is certain is that it was complied before 443 A.D. when the first Chinese translation is reported to have been attempted. But this does not mean that the whole text as we have it was then already in existence, for we know that the later translations done in 513 and 700-714 contain the Dharani and the Sagāthakam section which were missing in the 443 one.[9]

This ambiguous reference probably does not refer to the author of the *Nītiśāstra* in question but it is a very important Buddhist reference which may have helped justify the inclusion of such a non-Buddhistic text within the Tibetan Buddhist *bsTan 'Gyur*. The association of the name Masūrākṣa with some important *ṛṣi* of the future may have made anything associated with the name sacred for Buddhists.

Although the available references in Sanskrit literature are not very useful in the task of finding information about Masūrākṣa, Tibetan sources do provide some information. Around 1608 Kun-dga'-sñiṅ-po, who is better known as Tāranātha, wrote his famous *dGos-'dod-kun-byuṅ* (That Which Fulfills All Desires) which itself is better known as *rGya-gar-chos-'byuṅ (History of the Dharma in India).*[10] Tāranātha mentions someone named Masūrākṣita who was the son-in-law of the famous Pāla king Dharmapāla. After the death of Dharmapāla, Masūrākṣita seems to have taken over as regent during the minority of Dharmapāla's son Vanapāla.

> de'i rjes la ma su rakshi ta ces pa rgyal po dharma pa'a la'i mag pa cig gis rgyal srid lo brgyad tsham byas.[11]
>
> Then a King named Masūrākṣita who was the son-in-law of Dharmapāla ruled for eight years.

There is also mention of a Masūrākṣi near the beginning of the list of Pāla kings in Tāranātha's work.

> Ma su ra kshi tsha na ka/ gzhon skyon bzod pa
> skyon ba rnams/ pa'a la'i gseb la thor bur byuṅ[12]
>
> Masūrākṣi, Tsanaka (Cāṇakya), gShon-sKyon (Patra Pāla), and bZod-pa Skyon-pa (Kṣantipāla), were all individuals (who ruled) between (the reigns) of the Pālas.

The names Masūrākṣi, Masūrākṣita, and Masūrākṣa are undoubtedly the same. As the regent, Masūrākṣita may also have been in charge of the education of his young brother-in-law Vanapāla. Dharmapāla undoubtedly thought that Masūrākṣa would care for the kingdom and for the education of the young prince Vanapāla. The *Nītiśāstra* in question could very well have been one that Masūrākṣa assembled for the task of educating Vanapāla both in practical wisdom and in the affairs of kingship. Indeed many of the verses are the sort which pertain to the qualities of a good king and his various servants.[13]

Masūrākṣa is also mentioned by Sum-pa-mkhan-po, or as he is sometimes called, Ye-ses-pal-djor, in his famous *Pag-sam-jon-zan.*[14]

> de rjes dharma pa'a la'i mag pa ma suraki
> tas rgyal srid lo brgyad daṅ/[15]
>
> Then Masūrākṣita, the son-in-law of
> Dharmapāla, ruled for eight years.

This is a slightly different wording of the same statement made by Tāranātha. Sum-mkhan-po wrote his history about 1747 A.D. and undoubtedly used Tāranātha as a source and thus this does not really add any new information about Masūrākṣa.

The association with the famous Pāla king, Dharmapāla, is useful for fixing the date of Masūrākṣa. "The long reign of the great King Dharmapāla (c770-810) marks the apogee of the Pāla Power."[16] These dates traditionally associated with Dharmapāla would place Masūrākṣa's regentship in the second decade of the ninth century. Since this dating is imprecise, a wider margin should be extended, so that, for the purposes of this study, Masūrākṣa will be placed in the first half of the ninth century. Being a Pāla ruler, Masūrākṣa would have lived in Bengal.

There was substantial interaction between Bengal and Tibet during the time of the Pāla kings. There are records of large gifts being sent to the Tibetan monarch by the Pālas in 755.[17] The Tibetan chronicles indicate that there was a steady stream of Indian Buddhists who traveled to Tibet from the Pāla kingdom in Bengal. Tāranātha mentions that during the reign of Masūrākṣa, the famous Buddhist monk Laṅka-rgyal-ba-bzaṅ-po was sent to Tibet from Vikramaśīla, the Buddhist center in Bengal which had been founded by Dharmapāla.[18] Thus the contact between Tibet and the Pāla kingdom of India was well established. The traditional Tibetan account of the cultural contact between India and Tibet describes a widespread interaction in the seventh century in conjunction with the spread of Buddhism to Tibet.

> According to this traditional account, Buddhism was introduced into Tibet during the lifetime of Srong bstan sgam po, who died in 649, and is held by all schools to be the founder of the Tibetan royal dynasty... His conversion was said to result from the influence of his two wives, a Nepalese Princess and a Chinese princess.[19]

There is not much evidence to support this traditional view but it probably does reflect the fact that there was some cultural interaction during this period with China to the east and India and Nepal to the south.

> The orthodox tradition cannot be taken as literally true... the chronicles do not appear to offer proof of a real conversion of King Srong bstan sgam po to Buddhism, or even of his profession of faith in it or active support for it, such as the orthodox tradition maintains. Events of this kind first happen in the time of Khri Srong lde brtsan (756-97?), well after the period of Srong bstan sgam po, and culminate in the founding of the monastery of bSam yas.[20]

Throughout this period between the reigns of Srong-bstan-sgam-po and Khri-srong-lde-brtsan there was a great deal of political maneuvering by the various factions which controlled the power in Tibet. At stake was the issue of whether to embrace Chinese culture or Indian culture.

> The kings themselves possessed relatively limited authority. Their office was surrounded by religious prestige, but in practice the priestly class of Bon, and the aristocracy, hindered their exercise of sovereignty... It is clear anyway that the conflict between the opposing groups of forces must have been very violent. Other powers were certainly at work in addition to the two parties in direct contest. China had watched the rise of Tibetan power with anxiety, seeing it a threat to her own expansion into Central Asia. She could scarcely remain indifferent to the events in Tibet. China sent a series of missionaries to Tibet, who were probably not exclusively concerned with matters of religion. So it came about that Tibet in the second half of the seventh century, after having conquered extensive territories in Central Asia, began to succumb more and more to the enchantment of Chinese culture.[21]

During this same period various elements of Indian culture were also playing a significant role in Tibet. According to the traditional account, King Sron-bstan-sgam-po sent one of his ministers, Thom-mi-Sambhoṭa, to India around the year 629 in order to study the Sanskrit language. Thom-mi-Sambhoṭa returned to Tibet and created the Tibetan alphabet which was modeled on a late Gupta script.[22] This traditional account is probably fairly accurate since the Tibetan language did not have a fixed orthography before the need arose to preserve Buddhist texts in the Tibetan language. This was a concern for Sron-bstan-sgan-po since his wives probably brought various scriptural texts with them from their native lands.

Throughout the period from the reign of Sron-bstan-sgam-po to the reign of Khri-srong-lde-brtsan, cultural elements from both China and India were introduced into Tibet along with the differing Buddhist approaches and philosophies from each of these two countries. The traditional story as reported by the Tibetan chroniclers is that the doctrinal controversies led to a winner-take-all debate during the reign of Khri-srong-lde-brtsan. The debate was probably a symbolic confrontation as well for the political forces within Tibet itself and the cultural differences between Chinese civilization and Indian civilization as they are influencing Tibetan culture.

> Faced with the ensuing outburst of doctrinal antagonism between adherents of Indian and Chinese Buddhism, the king decided to cut short the proceedings with a religious disputation, the kind of rhetorical and theological duel that was then in vogue in India and China; a duel which meant not merely disgrace and humiliation, but sometimes even death, for the loser.[23]

> Toward the end of the following century (between 792 and 794) there occurred the important debate between the pundit Kamalaśila, representing the Indian-Nepalese Buddhism, which was a mixture of the Indian Yogācāra and Mādhyamika, and the Chinese teacher (*hva śaṅ* or *Ho śaṅ*) known by the Sanskrit name Mahāyāna deva; who preached a doctrine of complete quetism and inactivity. According to the Tibetan accounts, Kamalaśila refuted the Chinese teacher. The teacher and his party acknowledged themselves vanquished and were expelled from Tibet by order of the king.[24]

The results of this debate probably were not as dramatic as the traditional accounts would lead us to believe.

> However, even the subsequent council at bSam yas (792-4), in which according to Tibetan sources the Hwa shang was defeated, could not bring the strife to an end.[25]

> According to Chinese tradition, the king would seem to have decided in favour of the Chinese. However, there are contradictions between the reports given in Tibetan and Chinese sources... The Indian school has gained the upper hand; in this the influx of new teachers must also have helped. This does not mean however that the defenders of the Ch'an school have vanished completely.[26]

In any case, the Chinese influence seemed to decline after the debate at bSam-yas and the Indian cultural influences seem to have increased.

The Indian monks who traveled to Tibet during the seventh, eighth, and first half of the ninth centuries were bearers and transmitters of Indian culture. They carried with them not only the accumulated traditions of Indian Buddhism but also their individual appreciation of Indian civilization which included their heritage of folklore. Folk wisdom in the form of *niti* was an important part of this heritage which was carried to Tibet. The Tibetans held Indian wisdom in high regard since India was the birthplace of the historical Buddha and Buddhism. Tibetan folk wisdom as in the form of proverbs was an important part of Tibetan literature.

> Tibetan literature is extremely extensive... Its oldest branch is certainly folklore, which existed throughout the whole period of Tibetan history from the time when Tibet had no script until the present period.[27]

The early period of cultural and textual interchange with India ended in the middle of the ninth century when a king who was antagonistic toward Buddhism persecuted the Buddhists.

> The period A.D. 841-978 represents a gap in the Buddhist doctrine, owing to Gklan-dar-nma's persecution. The Later Spread begins with the life of the lotsava Rin-chen-bzaṅ-po (b. 958). While many of the early translations were later recovered from one source or another, the oral lineages had been mostly wiped out... In this second period of translation a huge literature on Buddhist Tantra was translated into Tibetan along with an enormous amount of commentary and exegetical literature.[28]

During both of these periods of translation, the Tibetans worked closely with Indian Buddhists who had brought the texts from India and who were familiar with the language of the texts and the meaning of the texts. The translations were done in a very literal style with frequent phonetic transliterations of Sanskrit words. This method was different from the Chinese method of translating Buddhist texts, where the concepts were translated without preserving the exact wording of the Indian original. The Tibetan technique was based on teamwork between a Tibetan *lo-tsa-wa* (translator) and an Indian pundit. Although sometimes larger groups were employed, the basic translating team consisted of two scholars.

One such team of translators was Śakya-blo-gros and Dharmaśrībhadra who are given credit for the translation of the *Nītiśāstra* of Masūrākṣa.[29] Although we have no primary sources which provide dates for either of these men, we do have enough references to them and to the other translators they worked with to establish their period of work fairly accurately. Both of them are closely associated with Atiśa and Rin-chen-bzan-po. Both Atiśa and Rin-chen-bzaṅ-po are mentioned frequently in texts of Tibetan chroniclers such as *Chos-'byung* of Bu-ston[30] (fourteenth century), *Deb-ther-snon-po* of 'Gos-lo-tsa-wa-gzon-nu-dpal[31] (fifteenth century), *rGya-gar-chos-'byuṅ* of Tāranātha (early seventeenth century), and *Pag-sam-jon-zang* of Sum-pa-mkhan-po (eighteenth century).

> Notwithstanding the uncertainties about our knowledge of some of the details of the life and activities of Dīpaṁkāra Śrījñana—alias Atiśa—his importance in the religious history of India and Tibet is, on the whole, clear and unmistakable. He was in fact a landmark in both,—being about the last of the great Buddhist ācāryas in India and, though not the first, he is remembered in Tibetan tradition itself as by far the greatest of the teacher-reformers of Tibet.[32]

Bu-ston reports that King Byaṅ-chob-'od instructed five monks under the leadership of Gya-tson-du-seṅ-ge to invite some important Buddhist scholar from India to aid in their translation project.[33]

> Accordingly, they invited Dīpaṃkāraśrījñana who was the son of Kalyāṇaśrī, the King of Bengal, and who had received a brilliant education at the monastery of Vikramaśila.[34]

After he arrived in Tibet one of his first visits seems to have been to the great translator Rin-chen-bzaṅ-po.

> When they came to the sleeping chamber of the great translator Rin-chen-bzaṅ-po, the latter first made his

> salutation, and then the Pundit addressed a hymn of praise to each of the images of the Tantric deities that were in the translator's room. The great translator was delighted, and they held together many discussions on religious questions. The translator again made his salutations and prayed to expound the Doctrine. After that they made numerous translations, and especially put in order the texts of the Yoga-tantra in accordance with the explanations of Anandagarbha and added numerous instructions to them.[35]

Bu-ston, however, fails to provide dates which could be used to solve the problem of the date of translation of the *Nītiśāstra* of Masūrākṣa.

The *Deb-ther-non-po*, or the *Blue Annals* as it is better known, contains a great deal of information about Atiśa including various anecdotes and provides the important information about dates. According to 'Gos-lo-tsa-wa, Atiśa was born "in the Water-Male-Horse year (chupho-'brug-982 A.D.)"[36] and died "on the twentieth day of the middle month of the year Wood-Male-Horse (siṅ-pho-rta—1054 A.D.),[37]

'Gos-lo-tsa-wa reports that Atiśa arrived in Tibet "in the year Water-Male-Horse (chu-pho-rta—1042 A.D.)"[38] Atiśa spent the next twelve years traveling around all parts of Tibet teaching and translating various manuscripts. In the *Blue Annals* his meeting with Rin-chen-bzaṅ-po is reported in the same manner as it was by Bu-ston, although 'Gos-lo-tsa-wa says that at the time of this meeting Rin-chen was eighty-five years old.[39] 'Gos-lo-tsa-wa also adds the significant information that 'Śakya-blo-gros was among Atiśa's tibetan disciples.[40] Tāranātha and Sum-pa do not add anything of significance to these data although Sum-pa does have more detail on the life of Rin-chen-bzaṅ-po.

Atiśa's work in Tibet was important for many reasons. He translated some of the major texts and provided commentaries for others. His teaching in various parts of Tibet helped spread his interpretations of Buddhism and one of the major sects of Tibetan Buddhism was founded upon his teachings.

> Atiśa himself founded no school or sect in Tibet, and his pupil 'Brom-ston (1005-64) was regarded as the leading personality from which that sect derived whose beliefs accorded most closely with the traditions of Atiśa. This sect received the name bKa-gdams-pa because, according to Sum-pa mkhan-po, it held fast to the authoritative word

(bka-gdams) of Atiśa as laid down primarily in his work *Lamp for the Way of Enlightenment.*

Atiśa was also important as a transmitter of Indian culture in his travels around Tibet. It is very possible that he was the one who brought the *Nītiśāstra* of Masūrākṣa from Vikramaśīla to Tibet since it was one of the Tibetan monks who is named as a disciple of Atiśa's who worked on the translation. Even if Atiśa had not brought the *Nītiśāstra* of Masūrākṣa to Tibet, his close association with Rin-chen-bzhaṅ-po, who is credited with having translated two of the other seven *nītiśāstras* in the *bsTan 'Gyur*,[42] and with his disciple Śakya-blo-gros, who is credited with working on the translation of Masūrākṣa *Nītiśāstra*, indicates that he was involved with those who were working with *nīti* verses.

Examining the list of works that were translated by both Śakya-blo-gros and Dharmaśrībhadra provides further evidence that these two enjoyed a close relationship with both Atiśa and Rin-chen-bzaṅ-po. (See chart 2.1). This association with Atiśa would indicate that the *Nītiśāstra* was probably translated into Tibetan somewhere around the middle of the eleventh century. The fact that Rin-chen-bzaṅ-po is also listed as being the translator of two of the other *lugs-kyi-bstan-chos* included in the *bsTan-'gyur* indicates that Rin-chen-bzaṅ-po felt that these *nīti* texts were of significance.

The several references in Sanskrit and Tibetan sources that concern Masūrākṣa and the translation of his *Nītiśāstra* into Tibetan provide us with enough information to make some meaningful speculations. It appears that Masūrākṣa was a member of the Pāla royal family by marriage and that he lived in Bengal in the first half of the ninth century A.D. His manuscript of *nīti* verses was carried to Tibet some time before the middle of the eleventh century, when it was translated into Tibetan by the *lo-tsa-wa* Śakya-blos-gros and the Indian pundit Dharmaśrībhadra and included in the mass of translations which were to become the *bsTan 'Gyur*. The *Nītiśāstra*, as a piece of non-Buddhist literature, represents the broad cultural interaction which was taking place between India and Tibet.

Notes

1. *sDe dGe bsTan 'Gyur mDo*. Bundle No 137b6-143a7 (Harvard Yenching Library Collection).
2. *Ibid.*, end of first chapter, 138a7-138b1.

3. P. Peterson (Editor), *The Subhāsitāvali of Vallebhadeva* (Bombay: Education Society's Press, 1886).
4. B. Nanjio (Editor), *The Lankāvatāra Sūtra* (Kyoto: Otani University Press, 1923.
5. Peterson, *Subhāṣitāvali*, p. 87.
6. *Ibid.*, verses 1306, 1491, 1344, 2805, 2758, 2684, 2734, 2759, 2816, 2757, and 2756 also occur in Masūrākṣa's *Nītiśāstra.*
7. This is verse number 3.35 in PP and verse number 3.43 in PKB.
8. Nanjio, *The Lankāvatāra Sūtra*, Verse 816, p. 367.
9. D.T. Suzuki (Trans), *The Lankāvatāra Sūtra* (London: Routledge and Kegan Paul, Ltd., 1932), p. xlii.
10. A. Schiefner (Editor), *Tranathae de Doctrinae Buddhicae in India Propagatione* (Petropoli: Eggers et socii, 1868).
11. *Ibid.*, p. 171.
12. *Ibid.*, p. 2.
13. The entire seventh chapter of Masūrākṣa's work except for the foma; verse concerns the king and his servants.
14. S.C. Das (Trans), *Pag Sam Jon Zang. History of the Rise, Progress, and Downfall of Buddhism in India by Sumpa Khan-po yese Pal Jor* Calcutta: Presidency Jail Press, 1908).
15. *Ibid.*, p. 114.
16. A. Basham, *The Wonder That Was India* (London: Sedgewick and Jackson, 1954), p. 70.
17. R.A. Stein, *Tibetan Civilization* (Stanford L: Stanford University Press, 1972), p. 64.
18. R.C. Majumdar (Editor), *The History and Culture of the Indian People* (Bombay: Bharatiya Vidya Bhavan, 1955), p. 49.
19. G. Tucci, *The Religion of Tibet*, Trans. G. Samuel (Berkeley: University of California Press, 1980), p. 1.
20. *Ibid.*, p. 2
21. *Ibid.*, p. 3-4.
22. A Wayman (Trans), *Calming the Mind and Discerning the Real* (New York: Columbia University Press, 1978), p. 4.
23. Stein, *Tibetan Civilization*, p. 67.
24. Wayman, *Calming the Mind*, p. 5.
25. Tucci, *Religions*, p. 6.
26. *Ibid.*, p. 13-14.
27. H. Hoffann, *Tibet, A Handbook* (Bloomington: Indiana University Press, 1975), p. 193.
28. Wayman, *Calming the Mind*, p. 5-6.
29. *sDe dGe bsTan 'Gyur mDo*, Ṅo 143a7.
30. E. Obermiller (Trans), *History of Buddhism (Chos-ḥayang) by Bu-ston* (Heidelberg; Otto Harrassowitz, 1931).
31. G. Roerich (Trans), *The Blue Annals* (Calcutta: Royal Asiatic Society of Bengal, 1949-53).
32. A. Chattopadhyaya, *Atiśa and Tibet* (Calcutta: Indian Studies Past and Present, 1967), p. 331.
33. Obermiller, *Bu-ston*, p. 213.
34. *Ibid.*, p. 213.
35. *Ibid.*, p. 214.
36. Roerich, *The Blue Annals*, p. 247.
37. *Ibid.*, p. 261.

38. *Ibid.*, p. 247.
39. *Ibid.*, p. 250.
40. *Ibid.*, p. 262.
41. H. Hoffmann, *The Religions of Tibet*, Trans, E. Fitzgerald (New York: The MacMillan Company, 1961), p. 132.
42. D. Suzuki (Editor), *The Tibetan Tripitika. Peking Edition Catalogue and Index* (Tokyo: Suzuki Research Foundation, 1962). The other two texts are the *Dri ma med pa'i dris lan rin po che'i phreṅ ba zes bya ba (Vimalapraśnottara ratnamālā nāma* of Amoghavarsa) and the *Tsa na ka'i rgyal po'i lugs kyi bstan bcos* (Cāṇakya rāja nītiśāstra).

3

Masūrākṣa did not cite the individual sources from which he drew the verses for his compilation. Therefore it is impossible to know for certain what materials, oral traditional and written, he had at his disposal. In verse 1.1, Masūrākṣa claims that he collected them from "various *śāstras* of *artha*" (*don gyi bstan bcos bye bdrag*)[1]. Such a statement seems to indicate that he used primarily written manuscripts or fixed mnestic texts for his sources rather than gathering the verses from an active oral tradition. He may have made use of an active oral tradition, but since there is no way this can be traced, speculation on the matter is useless. Masūrākṣa may have composed some of the verses himself but once again there is no concrete evidence of this. The peculiar structure of verses 1.3-1.12 may be an indication that Masūrākṣa composed these particular verses. These verses do not follow the general tendency of *nīti* verses to express a single thought or a consistent comparison of several things or actions. In most of these verses each line expresses an idea independent of the other three lines. If, in fact, Masūrākṣa had intended the work to be for the instruction of Prince Vanapāla, it is possible that this section at the beginning of the work could have been for the purpose of illustrating various grammatical constructions. However, without the Sanskrit original such a speculation cannot be supported. Since verse 1.1 follows the form of verses which introduce other collections of *nīti* verses such as CNI,[2] it is possible that this introductory verse is not as significant as it may appear.

The *śāstras* of *artha* which Masūrākṣa acknowledges as his sources could have been almost any pieces of literature that dealt with *artha* or *nīti*. *Śāstras* of *artha* would not be limited to mere treatises about *artha*, such as the *Arthaśāstra*, but could be considered to be all types of literature which were concerned with *artha*, including the vast Indian narrative tradition. The *Mahābhārata*, the *Pañcatantra*, and other narrative works were full of *artha* and *nīti* verses. Masūrākṣa undoubtedly had at his disposal various narratives and collections of verses which are not available to modern scholars. For example, collections of verses such as Masūrākṣa was to produce may have been common. Personal collections of this type may have been available to Masūrākṣa but afterwards for one reason or another they were not recopied as their manuscripts decayed and were not saved from extinction by the Tibetans as his was.

Since many of the sources that were available to Masūrākṣa in ninth century Bengal may have been lost as a result of not being recopied, it is difficult to know what the *śāstras* of *artha* were which he used. All that is possible is to track down the places these same verses occur in the pieces of literature which have survived. This will, of course, not necessarily indicate the sources which Masūrākṣa used, but these works can be viewed as common repositories of the verses in question. The end result of such speculations will be as clear a picture as possible of the resources available to Masūrākṣa from which he probably drew both his material and his inspiration. For the purposes of this study, the following sources have been examined in detail: the Cāṇakya Compendia as reconstructed from various manuscripts and printed texts by Ludwik Sternbach;[3] the *Pañcatantra*;[4] the *Mahābhārata*;[5] the *Hitopadeśa*;[6] and the *Garuḍa Purāṇa*.[7] Chart 3.1 lists the verses included by Masūrākṣa which also appear in one or more of the Cāṇakya collections (as classified by Sternbach), in one or more recensions of the *Pañcatantra*, in the *Mahābhārata* (Critical Edition), in one or more recensions of the *Hitopadeśa*, and in the *Garuḍa Purāṇa*. There is no real way of knowing which, if any, of these sources, Masūrākṣa may have used but most scholars at least agree that these particular sources were available in ninth century India. Many of these same verses also occur in sources which are considered or known to have been compiled after the period in which it appears Masūrākṣa lived. Appearances of these verses in some of the major post-Masūrākṣan sources have also been cited in order to show the persistent nature and popularity of the verses themselves. The major sources in this group are Vallabhadeva's *Subhāṣitāvali* (especially the *Nītipadhati*),[8] *The Paddhati of Śārṅgadhara*,[9] Sāyana's *Subhāṣita-Sudhānidhi*,[10] the *Subhāṣitaratnākara*,[11] the *Subhāṣita-ratna-bhāṇḍāgāra*,[12] Bohtlingk's *Indische Spruche*,[13] and Sternbach's *Mahāsubhāṣita Saṃgraha*.[14]

The period of the Pāla Dynasty, in which Masūrākṣa appears to have played a minor role, was one of artistic and literary activity which included an awareness of the cultural heritage and an appreciation of the literary tradition of Bengal.

The reign of the Pāl kings lasted over three hundred years,

> and it is justly noted for its cultural achievements. Bengali language and literature are generally supposed to have been born in the Pāl period and the stone and cast-metal sculpture of that period is well known.[15]
>
> It was under the Pālas that new forms of Sanskrit literature were invented, and together with this broadening of the Sanskrit tradition went an enthusiasm for its literature that brought about the exchange of manuscripts between Bengal and western India, the exchange of translations between Bengal and Tibet, perhaps even between Bengal and the islands of Indonesia.[16]

The Pāla kings patronized various religions as well as the arts and under the Pālas the Buddhist center of learning at places such as Vikramaśīla prospered. The monastery at Vikramaśīla is of particular importance to the spread of Buddhism to Tibet for it was from Vikramaśīla that many of the monks who were to participate in the Tibetan translation project including Atiśa himself set out.

> The ninth century was the golden age of Bengali Sanskrit poetry. This was the century of Yogeśvara and Abhinanda. This was the century when Pāla authors broadened the Sanskrit tradition to include descriptions of peasants and beggars as well as kings and *nāyikās*.[17]

Although the Bengali language is generally believed to have originated during the Pāla period, many writers still made extensive use of Sanskrit.

> The prestige of Sanskrit was greater than even after Kalidasa and the other writers of the classical period had enriched it with their genius. Then there was a decline, but Sanskrit was still the cultural language when Bengali was born in the days of the Pāl and Sen Kings. Poets of genius such as Jayadeva, and aspirants after fame, influence, and favour, would still write in Sanskrit and not in Bengali. They did so not only because Sanskrit was the better language, but for the natural desire they had to belong to the great tradition Sanskrit embodied.[18]

Thus it is not unusual that Masūrākṣa would have written his *Nītiśāstra* in Sanskrit rather than in Bengali. In the opening statement of the Tibetan translation, Śakya-blos-gros and Dharmaśrībhadra give the original Sanskrit title as simply *Nītiśāstra (rgya gar skad du ni ti sha stra)*[19] so it is certain that the manuscript used by the Tibetans was in Sanskrit.

Problems with the preservation of manuscripts in Bengal, as in most of India, were prime factors in the compilation of *nītiśāstras* and *subhāṣita saṃgrahas* in general.

> Alas for the climate of Bengal! Its white ants have eaten and its monsoons have mildewed the records of its enlightened past.[20]

Although many of the individual verses for the collections of verses came out of oral traditional material, the whole corpus of oral traditional narrative was too vast to set down in writing and copy over again and again. Only the most popular or most significant narratives were committed to manuscripts and preserved by periodic reproduction. Preservation problems of this type also helped maintain the oral traditional process since the only access the common Indian would have to the vast narrative corpus would be through oral traditional means. The importance of the wisdom contained in the *nīti* verses from these oral traditional narratives justified committing the verses themselves to writing and then recopying them as it became necessary. Smaller collections gradually became incorporated into larger collections or were lost entirely, as Masūrākṣa's collection would have been had not the Tibetans rescued it from oblivion. Many of the smaller collections of *nıti* and *artha* verses lost their association with individual compilers and became associated with the legendary master of didactic verse, Caṇakya. This may have served to have given added rationalization to the need to preserve the verses as a result of the reverence in which the name Cāṇakya was held.

Although an oral tradition was probably the spawning ground for most *nīti* verses, there is no means of documenting the process by which the verses were composed or used in oral presentation. All that is available today are the manuscripts and printed texts of narratives which make use of these bits of folk wisdom and the collections of such verses generally associated with the name of Cāṇakya.

> Although the collections of Cāṇakya's wise sayings possess a fairly old traditional nucleus, many of these aphorisms also occur in other works of Sanskrit literature, such as epics, purāṇa-s, *dharmaśāstra-s, kāvya-s, kathā-s*, and others. This identity does not imply direct borrowing from each

> other, because the floating mass of oral tradition may have served as a common depository for those borrowings.[21]

The collections of verses ascribed to Cāṇakya are not rare and many different manuscripts and printed texts of these verses exist today. Ludwik Sternbach's work of cataloging and classifying these Cāṇakya collections has been invaluable. His assumption that all existing texts can be organized into one of six basic versions is not sound, since, in order to do this, he has to disregard many individual verses which are as legitimate as the ones he chooses to include in his Urtexts. Chart 3.2 lists the verses included by Masūrākṣa which also appear in one or more of the Cāṇakya versions as cataloged by Sternbach. Unfortunately Sternbach does not list the verses he rejects in the *Cāṇakya-Nīti-Text-Tradition*. Presumably these verses will eventually appear in the *Mahāsubhāṣita Samgraha* which is currently being assembled under his guidance.

One of the earliest narrative sources of *nīti* verse is the *Pañcatantra*. The stories themselves are undoubtedly almost straight out of a very active oral tradition in India. They have all the earmarks of oral traditional construction including several significant multiforms. Comparison with the tales in the Buddhist Jātaka section of the Pali Tripitika indicates a great many similarities.[22] The point at which the basic oral traditional tales which included the *nīti* verses were committed to writing is questionable. The first written versions of the *Pañcatantra* have not survived, so it is impossible to know the point at which they were first put into written form. One date that is fairly well established in connection with these early versions of the *Pañcatantra* is the date at which a version of the *Pañcatantra* was translated into Pahlevi, about 570 A.D.[23] No copies of this translation have survived but later translations which claim to have been made from this Pahlevi translation exist in Syriac and Arabic.

> The Arabic translation of the Pahlevi text was the source from which sprang all the subsequent translations and adaptations in the languages of Europe and Asia either directly or indirectly.[24]

Chart 3.3. lists the verses included by Masūrākṣa which also appear in one or more of the versions of the *Pañcatantra*.

The *Mahābhārata*, which seems to have had its roots in oral tradition, also contains many of the verses used by Masūrākṣa. At some indeterminable point manuscripts were produced from oral performances of the story of the adventures of the Pāṇḍavas and the Bhārata War. The popularity and spread of the Kṛṣṇa Cult in India may have helped create a demand for access to the epic since it could be used as a vehicle to embody cult viewpoints.[25] The section of the sixth book which become known as the *Bhagavad Gīta* was especially significant to the proponents of the cult. The widespread popularity of the *Mahābhārata* as an oral traditional narrative as well as the fact that Kṛṣṇa played a part in the action made it very attractive for cultic purposes. The *Mahābhārata* was also supportive of Brahmin supremacy in general and thus the learned Brahmins who controlled the manuscript copies had a definite stake in its preservation and its "improvement" (i.e. the clarifying of vague or inadequate information in accordance with their beliefs). Over the years the various manuscripts of the *Mahābhārata* gradually evolved in response to the needs of the Brahmins who controlled the manuscripts. There is no way of knowing when the mass of *nīti* verses contained in the *Mahābhārata* was included. Many of the individual ones such as Vidura's statement in 2.55.10[26] are common *nīti* maxims and were probably part of the original oral traditional version. It seems likely that the larger blocks of verses such as MBh 5.35.40[27] and MBh 12.138[28] were added during one of the many changes to the original manuscripts. Chart 3.1 lists the verses included by Masūrākṣa which also appear in the Critical Edition of the *Mahābhārata*.

Another possible source of verses for Masūrākṣa was the *Hitopadeśa* which is believed to have been composed in Bengal around the ninth century just as the *Nītiśāstra* of Masūrākṣa appears to have been.

> Thus there is an accumulation of persuasive evidence that Nārāyana was a Bengali and that he wrote his *Hitopadeśa* in Eastern Bengal.[29]
>
> So if we place Nārāyaṇa between A.D. 800 and 900 (or at the very latest 950), I think there is little chance of our being wrong.[30]

There is no way of knowing whether or not the *Hitopadeśa* was available to Masūrākṣa but since there are seventeen verses which appear both in Masūrākṣa's collection and the *Hitopodeśa*, such a speculation is worth considering. Since Nārāyaṇa acknowledges use of the *Pañcatantra* for his composition of the *Hitopadeśa*, some of these verses may have come directly out of the *Pañcatantra*. Six of the verses used by

Masūrākṣa which are common to the *Hitopadeśa* are not found in the *Pañcatantra* (see chart 3.1) and thus it seems very likely that Masūrākṣa also had access to Nārāyaṇa's work. Since Masūrākṣa probably produced his *Nītiśāstra* during the first half of the ninth century, this would push the date of the composition of the *Hitopadeśa* back to the early part of the period mentioned above. Chart 3.4 lists the verses included by Masūrākṣa which appear in one or more of the recensions of the *Hitopadeśa*.

The *Bṛhaspati-saṃhita* of the *Garuḍa Purāṇa* also contains a great many verses in common with Masūrākṣa's collection.

> The *Garuḍa-purāṇa*, as most of the Purāṇa-s, is not a uniform work; it is a work of encyclopaedic character containing almost everything of general interest... it appears that the *Garuḍa-purāṇa* is the work of different specialists, a jumble of quite loosely connected mass of contents designed and contemplated to make it on the one hand a religious manual for the Smarta priests, and on the other hand, a popular handbook for every sort of popular information.[31]

Little is known about the compilation of the *Garuḍa Purāṇa* although the *Bṛhaspati-saṃhita* is basically a collection of *nīti* verses.

> To what exact age the encyclopaedic work, known as the *Garuda-purāṇa* belongs is difficult to say, for this Purāṇa is the outcome of so many heterogeneous compilations from different standard works, that no particular century will probably cover the series of widely different dates, in which the respective parts of this Purāṇa came into being... But... the GP in our present form was probably compiled between 850 and 1000 A.D.[32]

Sternbach feels that the Bṛhaspati-saṃhita is in reality merely a version of what he terms the *Cāṇakya-Rāja-Nīti-Śastra*.[33] Again there is some question as to whether or not Masūrākṣa could have had access to the *Garuḍa Purāṇa* but there are thirty-three verses which appear in both Masūrākṣa's collection and the *Garuḍa Purāṇa*. Only one of these verses does not appear in the *Cāṇakya-Rāja-Nīti-Śāstra* as Sternbach has reconstructed it, so it is possible that Masūrākṣa used the *Cāṇakya-Rāja-Nīti-Śāstra* rather than the *Garuḍa Purāṇa*. Chart 3.1 lists the verses included by Masūrākṣa which also appear in the *Garuḍa Purāṇa*.

The presence of verses used by Masūrākṣa in texts which were compiled or composed after the period during which Masūrākṣa worked is a positive indicator of the popularity and the importance of the individual verses. There is the chance as well that one or more of the compilers of these *saṁgrahas* had access to a manuscript of Masūrākṣa's *Nītiśāstra*. Chart 3.5 lists the verses included by Masūrākṣa which also appear in Vallabhadeva's *Subhāṣitāvali, The Paddhati of Śārṅgadhara*, the *Subhāṣitaratnākara*, Sāyana's *Subhāṣita-Sudhānidhi*, the *Subhāṣita-ratna-bhāṇḍāgāra*, Bŏhtlingk's *Indische Sprüche*, and Sternbach's *Mahāsubhāṣita-Saṃgraha*.

Unfortunately only one of these post-Masūrākṣan sources mentions Masūrākṣa by name. Vallabhadeva gives Masūrākṣa credit for verse number 2935 in his *Subhāṣitāvali*, although, as has been mentioned, this is also a common verse from the *Pañcatantra*. There are also eleven other verses that are common to both Masūrākṣa and Vallabhadeva (see Chart 3.5) which Vallabhadeva does not identify with Masūrākṣa or anyone else for one reason or another.

> A very well known *subhāṣita-saṃgraha* is Vallabhadeva's *subhāṣitāvali*. We do not know very much about the author and the question of its dating gave rise to long discussions. It is generally accepted, however, that this anthology, in the form in which it is available, today, cannot have been compiled earlier than the fifteenth century.[34]

If, in fact, Vallabhadeva had access to a manuscript of Masūrākṣa's work as late as the fifteenth century, then this would tend to indicate that Masūrākṣa's *Nītiśāstra* was popular enough to have been preserved for at least 600 years. The possibility exists that some intermediary compiler quoted the verse in question as being one of Masūrākṣa's but since we have no access to such an intermediary, we can only assume that Masūrākṣa's works were available to Vallabhadeva. The *Paddhati* of Śārṅgadhara is believed to have been compiled in the fourteenth century and could potentially be such an intermediary.[35] Chart 3.5 indicates that there are only eight verses included by Śārṅgadhara which also appear in the collection of Masūrākṣa. All eight of these verses also appear in various Cāṇakya collections as well. Four of these verses are used by Vallabhadeva but verse 2935, which Vallabhadeva has identified with the name of Masūrākṣa, is not one of these. Thus it appears that Vallabhadeva quotes Masūrākṣa independently of Śārṅgadhara.

Another fourteenth century collection of *nīti* verses which could potentially be an intermediary source between Masūrākṣa and Vallabhadeva is the *Subhāṣita-Sudhānidhi* of Sāyana.[36] Chart 3.5 shows that seven of the fourteen verses which Sāyana has in common with Ṃasūrākṣa are also verses included by Vallabhadeva. Verse 2935 which Vallabhadeva ascribes to Masūrākṣa is included in Sāyana's collection but Sāyana does not assign Masūrākṣa's name to the verse. Thus it seems unlikely that Vallabhadeva used Sāyana as an intermediary source.

Collections of *subhāṣita*-s became very popular during the last half of the nineteenth century and several of these collections include a quantity of verses which Masūrākṣa included in his *Nitiśāstra.*

> During the second half of the nineteenth and twentieth century India was inundated by modern *subhāṣita-saṃgraha*-s many of which were edited as textbooks of Sanskrit to be used at schools, and also preserve "ancient thoughts" and "Ancient moral teachings." The most complete and carefully edited in the *Subhāṣita-ratna-Bhāṇḍāgāram* by Nārāyaṇa Rāma Ācārya "Kāvyatīrtha"...It is the most complete modern *subhāṣita*-saṃgraha.[37]

Chart 3.5 indicates that the *Subhāṣita-ratna-bhāṇḍāgāra* has thirty-five verses in common with Masūrākṣa's collections. Another late nineteenth century compilation of *subhāṣita-s* is the *Subhāṣitaratnākara* that was edited by Krishna Śāstri Bhātavadekar in 1888. There are seven verses common to both Masūrākṣa's work and the *Subhāṣitaratnākara.*

Otto Bŏhtlingk's *Indische Sprüche* and Ludwik Sternbach's *Mahāsubhāṣita Saṃgraha* are the two best collections of Sanskrit *subhāṣitas* made by westerners that have western translations accompanying the verses. Bŏhtlingk's three volume series, which appeared between 1870 and 1873 complete with a German translation of each verse, has fifty-four of the verses which Masūrākṣa included. All of these fifty-four verses appear in one or more of the other sources that have been considered above. Sternbach's collection is still in progress. There is an English translation with each Sanskrit verse.

Masūrākṣa included many verses that also appear in various "*śāstras of artha*" which were available to him as charts 3.1-3.4 illustrate. Of the one hundred twenty-four verses in the *Nītiśāstra* sixty-six or fifty-three percent can be seen to have come directly from the sources we still have available today. If the ten verses in the first section are not included since they appear to have been written or at least put in their present form by Masūrākṣa, then fifty-eight percent of the remaining verses can be shown to have existed in some form during the ninth century which is still available today.

Notes

1. *sDe dGe bsTan 'Gyur mDo*. Bundle Ṅo. 137b6-143a7 (Harvard Yenching Library Collection), Folio 137b7. Verse 1.1.
2. Ludwik Sternbach, *The Cāṇakya-Nīti-Text-Tradition*, Vol. 2, Part 2 (Hoshiarpur: Visveshvaranand Vedic Research Institute, 1967), p. 159.
3. Sternbach, *The Cāṇakya-Nīti-Text-Tradition*, 2 Vols.
4. Six recensions of *The Pañcatantra* were consulted for the purposes of this dissertation. As cited in the abbreviation list, these are PKB, PP, PRE, PS, PT and PTK.
5. V.S. Sukthankar (Editor). *The Mahābhārata-Critical Edition* (Poona: Bhandarkar Oriental Research Institute, 1933-59).
6. Six recensions of *The Hitopadeśa* were consulted for the purposes of this dissertation. As cited in the abbreviation list, these are HH, HJ, HK, HM, HP, and HS.
7. R. Bhattacharya (Editor), *Garuḍapurāṇaṁ* (Varanasi: Chaukhambha Sanskrit Sansthan, 1964).
8. P. Peterson (Editor). *The Subhāṣitāvali of Vallabhadeva* (Bombay: Education Society's Press, 1886).
9. P. Peterson (Editor). *The Paddhati of Sārṅgadhara* (Bombay: Government Central Book Depot, 1888).
10. K. Krishnamoorty (Editor). *Sāyana's Subhāṣita-Sudhānidhi* (Dharwar: Karnatak University, 1968).
11. Kṛṣṇa Sastry Bhatavadekar (Editor), *Subhāṣitaratnākara* (Bombay: Gopal Narayen and Co., 1888).
12. K.P. Paraba (Editor), *Subhāṣita-Ratna-Bhāṇḍāgāra* (Bombay: Nirnayasagara Press, 1886).
13. O. Bŏhtlingk (Editor), *Indische Sprüche* (St. Petersberg: Eggers et Co., 1870-3).
14. Ludwik Sternbach (Editor), *The Mahāsubhāṣita Saṃgraha* (Hoshiarpur: Vishveshvaranand Vedic Research Institute, 1974-). Only three volumes were available from the Library of congress so far.
15. J.C. Ghosh, *Bengali Literature* (London: Oxford University Press, 1948_, p. 5.
16. D.H.H., Ingalls, "The Cāṇakya Collections and Nārāyana's Hitopadeśa" *Journal of the American Oriental Society* 96 (1966), p. 19.
17. *Ibid.*, p. 18.
18. Ghosh, *Bengali Literature*, p. 13.
19. *sDe dGe bsTan 'Gyur mDo*, folio 137b6.
20. Ingalls, "The Cāṇakya Collections," p. 18.
21. Ludwik Sternmbach, *Subhāṣita, Gnomic, and Didactic Literature* Wiesbaden: Otto Harrassowitz, 1974), p. 45.
22. H.T. Francis and E.J. Thomas (Editors), *Jātaka Tales*, (Cambridge: Cambridge University Press, 1916), p. 2.

23. M. Winternitz, *A History of Indian Literature*, Trans. S. Ketkar (Calcutta: University of Calcutta, 1927), p. 309.
24. *Ibid*., p. 334.
25. This view was expressed by Professor D.H.H. Ingalls in a lecture for Humanities 9a given February 28, 1980.
26. Mahābhārata-Critical Edition. 2.55.10
tyajet kulārthe puruṣaṃ grāmasyārthe kulaṃ tyajet
grāmaṃ janpadasyārthe ātmārthe pṛthivīṃ tyajet
27. This group of verses constitutes a discourse by Vidura in which he quotes a whole string of *nīti* verses.
28. This group of *nīti* verses is quoted by Bhisma as having been said by the *ṛshi* Bharadwaja.
29. Ingalls, "The Cāṇakya Collections," p. 10.
30. *Ibid*., p. 18.
31. Sternbach, *The Cāṇakya-Nīti-Text Tradition*, Vol., 1., part 2, p. Liii.
32. *Ibid*., p. Lvii.
33. L. Sternbach, "The Cāṇakya-Rāja-Nīti-Śāstra and the Bṛhaspati Sṃhita of The Garuḍa Purāṇa," *Annals of the Bhandarkar Oriental Research Institute*, 37 (1956), p. 69.
34. Sternbach, *Subhāṣita*, p. 22.
35. *Ibid*., p. 18-19.
36. *Ibid*., p. 19.
37. *Ibid*., p. 30.

4

In this chapter the individual verses chosen by Masūrākṣa will be examined. The format for examining each verse will be as follows: the Tibetan verse as found in the *bsTan 'Gyur*; the English translation of the Tibetan; a listing of the places where similar verses occur in Sanskrit literature; the Sanskrit prototype of the verse if possible; and explanatory notes when appropriate.

The Tibetan verse cited will be a critical composite taken from the four available versions of the Tibetan *bsTan 'Gyur*. These four versions are the *sNar Thang* edition,[1] the *sDe dGe* edition,[2] the *Peking* edition,[3] and the Cone edition.[4] Each of the versions was made from wood blocks which were cut during the eighteenth century.

> The first attempt to print the Tibetan cannon was made during the first part of the thirteenth century by ḥJam-nag-gab-sis, a disciple of mChom-ldan-rla-khri, who obtained funds from China for the purpose. The various masters such as Blo-gsal saṅs-rgyas ḥbum, Bsod-nams ḥod-zer, and Byaṅ-chub ḥbum, gathered together sūtras; vinaya texts, and tantric texts from various places, collated, and then printed them. Only then was the work (of putting the canon together) completed for the first time. This was known as the Snar-thaṅ old edition. The wood blocks as well as the printed copies of this edition are no longer available.[5]

The *sNar Thang* edition which is available today was based on this older version of the Tibetan canon which was put together at the sNar Thang monastery which was near the capital of western Tibet.[6]

> The oldest edition printed in Tibet was carved during the time of the Seventh Dalai Lama at sNar-thang where the blocks were also kept. The *bKa'-'gyur* was completed in 1731 and the *bsTan-'gyur* was completed in 1731 and the *bsTan-'gyur* in 1742, the first comprising 100, the latter 225 volumes

The *Peking* edition was carved a few years earlier in China.

> As for the Peking edition, work was commenced in the twenty-second year of K'ang-hsi (1683) in Peking, with the copy kept in the Sha-lu monastery as its basis. At first only the *Kanjur* was printed, but later, in the second year of Yung-Cheng (1724), the *Tanjur* was carved and printed.[8]

The *sDe dGe* edition was carved at the sDe-dGe monastery in Khams during the first half of the eighteenth century.

> The sDe-dge edition, which goes back to an older Lithang edition now lost, was printed in red ink in 1733 and was based on the Ming edition.[9]

The *Cone* edition is usually considered to be of the "sDe-dGe family" since it is nearly identical with the *sDe-dGe* edition.

> As for the Co-ne edition, its blocks are preserved in co-ne ch'inghai. though it is not known when these blocks were first carved, it is said to be after the Sde-dge edition.[10]

The Tibetan verse cited takes the readings which make the most sense from the four versions available. All variations are noted immediately following the chosen text (notations are by line number and word number within the line, e.g. 3.2 is the second word of the third line).

The English translation was made from the critical reading of each verse.

The next section for each individual verse lists the places where similar verses occur in Sanskrit literature. Subsection (1) contains occurrences of the verse in Sanskrit literature from sources which may have been available to Masūrākṣa. Subsection (2) contains occurrences of the verse in Sanskrit literature from sources which were compiled or composed after the period in which Masūrākṣa lived.

The probable Sanskrit original is given in the next section. Since *nīti* verses, being part of oral tradition, do not have a single fixed form the version which seems to be closest to the Tibetan wording is given in full. Variations from this chosen version are listed immediately following the chosen form. Variations are noted according to the *pāda* number in the verse.

The last section which is included for some of the verses is a section of notes which refer to some aspect of the Tibetan or Sanskrit verse as cited. These notes will often contain a translation of the

Sanskrit if it differs significantly from the Tibetan. The references to verses from Sanskrit sources are all to sources which are available at Harvard University or through interlibrary loan. Additional references of manuscripts and printed editions can be found by consulting L. Sternbach's *Cāṇakya-Nīti-Text Tradition.*[11]

1.1 don gyi bstan bcos bye brag las
bstan bcos bdag la phan pa daṅ
mi rnams blo ni bskyed bya'i phyir
ma su ra kshas bsdus te bshad

3.6 *sNar, Peking* pa'i

****

Having collected verses from various *śāstras* of *artha*, Masūrākṣa has related this *śāstra* for our benefit and for the sake of producing intelligence in men.

****

(1) Cr 587; CN avatarṇikā 1

****

Cr nānāśāstroddhṛtaṃ rājanītisamuccayam
sarvabījam idaṃ śāstraṃ cāṇakyaṃ sārasaṃgraham

****

The Tibetan verse makes Masūrākṣa the subject, but the idea is similar to Sanskrit introductory verses as cited.

1.2 'jig rten legs bskyed shes pa sbrag phyir daṅ
spyod pa ṅan pa rnams ni spaṅ phyir daṅ
Shes rab bslab phyir yaṅ dag don sgrub phyir
blo skyed phyir ni tshigs bcad tshul 'di brjod

1.3 *sDe, Cone* dag

1.4 *sDe, Cone* ni

1.5 *sDe, Cone* dga'a

1.6 *sDe, Cone* ba

1.7 *sDe, Cone* bskyed

1.8 *sDe, Cone* pa

1.9 *sNar* missing from text

3.4 *sDe, Cone* ciṅ

4.2 *snar, Peking* bskyed

4.5 *sNar, Peking* tshig

4.6 *sNar, Peking* bshad

Line 2 is missing from both the *sNar Thang* and the *Peking* editions of the *bsTan 'Gyur.*

****

For the sake of bringing together knowledge that produces good things in the world, for the sake of abandoning all evil deeds, for the sake of teaching this knowledge, for the sake of attaining one's aims, and for the sake of producing wisdom, I speak this manner of aphorism.

****

(1) Cr 406; CV 1.3; Cv 1.3; CS 1.3

****

Cr tad aham sampravakṣāmi lokānāṃ hitakāmyayā
yena vijñānamātrena sarvajñatvaṃ prapadyate

(b) Cv, CS narānāṃ

(c) CV yasya; CS prajñā pravarddhate

(d) CS māteva hitakāriṇī

****

The Tibetan verse contains more ideas on the motivation for the collection than does the Sanskrit verse but the basic idea is the same.

****

1.3 dṅos po kun la mkhas shiṅ goms par bya
chos spyad gzhan gyi mṅon sum bsruṅ bar bya
khro ba spaṅ zhiṅ mkhas po bsten par bya
bden par smra zhiṅ sgra nāms brjod mi bya

2.2. *sNar, Peking* spyod

2.5 *sNar, Peking* mṅen

3.5 *sNar, Peking* pa

****

Showing diligence in all matters, one should act; one should protect the vision of others who practice *dharma*; abandoning anger, one should show prudence; speaking the truth, one should not say vile things.

****

No similar verses were found is Sanskrit.

1.4 bram ze bkur zhiṅ ba laṅ brñas mi bya
rgyal bos 'jigs shiṅ spyod pa spa bar bya
dgra bos shes bya mi rnams brñas mi bya
dregs pa spaṅ zhiṇ smad dṅos bsten mi bya

1.5 *sDe, Cone* ṅan

1.6 *sDe, Cone* la'an

3.2 *sNar, Peking* bo

4.1 *sNar* drags

4.3 *sNar* spa

****

While honoring brahmins, one should not be disrespectful to cows; one who is afraid of a king should conceal his deeds; one should know one's enemies and not be disrespectful to any men; abandoning arrogance, one should not reveal vile characteristics.

****

No similar verses were found in Sanskrit.

1.5 phan pa'i zas bsten grogs po mñes par bya
me la mi 'gom gyul la blta mi bya
sñan ṅag mñan bya srog chags gnod mi bya
bya min mi bya khron pa bgom mi bya

1.7 *sNar, Peking* brñas

1.8 *sNar, Peking* mi

2.4 *sNar, Peking* bgom

3.4 *sNar, Peking* zhiṅ

****

By serving beneficial foods, one will delight his friends; by not walking on fire, one will avoid trouble; one should listen to poetry and not do harm to living things; one should not do that which is improper such as walking on the edge of a well.

****

No similar verses were found in Sanskrit.

1.6 rig pa blaṅ zhiṅ sbrul la tse mi bya
ci nus sbyin zhiṅ dman la bslad mi bya
bdag la mi bstod gzhan la smad mi bya
de ñid shes bya mtshan mo gryu mi bya

1.6 *sDe, Cone* daṅ

2.4 *sNar, Peking* zhan

2.7 *sNar, Peking* bslaṅ

3.1 *Cone* byad

3.2 *Cone* gal

****

Having attained knowledge, one will not seek out a serpent; giving according to one's ability, one should not give to an inferior person; not praising one's self, one should not slander others; one should know one's self and should not walk about at night.

****

No similar verses were found in Sanskrit.

1.7 zhags pa daṅ bran glaṅ po'i rjes mi 'gro
lham med mi 'gro grogs med lam mi 'gro
smyo byed blo ṅan riṅ du spaṅ bar bya
chuṅ ma ma ruṅs spaṅ zhin yid ' oṅ bsten

1.6 *sNar, Peking* la

****

One should not follow after a bull whose leash is disconnected; one should not walk without boots and one should not walk on a road without a friend; abandon to a distance evil advice that produces craziness; abandoning an unsuitable wife, one should depend upon an agreeable one.

****

No similar verses were found in Sanskrit.

1.8 ma 'dris pa daṅ nam yaṅ mthun mi 'jug
rgyal bo'i bran mo 'dod spaṅ man ṅag ñan
gaṅ daṅ lhan cig zhe 'gras yod mi bya
be'u gzhon pa drus riṅ du spaṅ bar bya

2.7 *sDe, Cone* ma'i

2.9 *sNar, Peking* mñan

3.6 *sNar, Peking* 'dus

4.4 *sDe, Cone* missing from text

****

One should not enter into association with those who are unfamiliar; one should heed the instruction to abandon the desire for the king's courtesan; one should avoid those whose disposition is quarrelsome; one should abandon to a distance a cow that is giving birth to a calf.

****

No similar verses were found in Sanskrit.

1.9 bud med rnams la nam yaṅ yid mi brtan
chu bo rgal dka'a rgya cher 'jug mi bya
chaṅ 'thuṅs ra ro shiṅ mthor 'dzeg mi bya
don rnams bsgrub ciṅ chos daṅ nor mi span

1.5 *Cone* rnam

2.3 *sNar, Peking* brgal

2.6 *Cone* tshar

3.7 *sNar, Peking* mdzeg; *Cone* 'jeg

****

One should not let one's mind be at all dependent upon women; one should note enter a river that is wide and hard to cross; being drunk on wine, one should not climb to the top of a tree; accomplishing one's aims, one should not abandon *dharma* and wealth.

****

No similar verses were found in Sanskrit.

1.10 gaṅ du bsruṅ ba med pa'i yul du spaṅ
kun gyi gsaṅ tshig nam yaṅ mi smra ste
kun la yid brtan mi bya legs par brtag
kha rjer mi gtad skyes bus rtsol ba 'bad

1.8 *sNar, Peking* de

1.9 *sDe, Cone* yaṅ

4.1 *sDe, Cone* kha

4.4 *sNar, Peking* bsded

4.6*sDe, Cone* bu'i

4.8 *sDe, Cone* la

Line 3 is missing from the texts of both the *sNar Thang* and the *Peking* editions of the *bsTan 'gyur.*

****

One should abandon a country in which there is no protection; one should never speak that word which is secret to everyone; one should not place confidence in anyone, only those who exhibit good traits; one should endeavor to seek a man who does not resort to changing his words.

****

No similar verses were found in Sanskrit.

1.11 gsoṅ bor smra zhiṅ 'brel med tshig mi brjod
glo bur lhags mdun dus su legs 'koṅs brjod
mi daṅ lha daṅ bram ze rnams la mchod
bsod nams yul ni rtag tu bsten par bya

1.1 *sDe, Cone* gsaṅ

1.6 *sNar, Peking* min

1.9 *sNar, Peking* smra

2.3 *sDe, Cone* lcag

3.9 *sNar, Peking* mchad

****

Speaking sincerely, one does not produce a word that is inconsistent; one should speak a welcome at the time of an unexpected arrival; one should honor men, gods, and brahmins; one should always visit holy places.

****

No similar verses were found in Sanskrit.

1.12 rtag tu khrus daṅ gos dkar gyon la 'grus
ha caṅ bud med chags min zhu nas za
shes ldan gaṅzhig de ltar byed pa ni
'tsho ba nad med tshe riṅ shes par bya

1.7 *sNar, Peking* gos

1.9 *sNar, Peking* gus

2.9 *sNar, Peking* bza'a

****

One should always bathe and then put on clean clothes; one should not cling too much to a woman; after asking permission, one should eat; anyone who possessing this knowledge acts accordingly will know a long life that is free from sickness.

****

No similar verses were found in Sanskrit.

2.1 bdag gis gsaṅ daṅ gzhan gyis gsaṅ
bu gcig gces bzhin bsruṅ bya ste
sa bzhin kun la sñoms byas nas
mi rnams dga'a bas rab tu dga'a

2.2 *sNar, Peking* bzhin

3.6 *sNar, Peking* par

3.7 *sNar, Peking* bya

****

One's own secrets and the secrets of others should be guarded as if they were beloved sons; considering everything as if it were dirt, men become very happy with joy.

****

No similar verses were found in Sanskrit.

2.2 gnad kyi tshig rnams mi brjod ciṅ
gnad du 'phog 'gyur mi bsgrags te
gzhan gyi gnad rnams smra ba ni
skyes bus mtshon cha bzhin zhes bya

2.3 *sDe, Cone* phog

2.6 *sNar, Peking* bsrag

2.7 *sNar, Peking* ste

3.6 *Peking* pa

4.6 *sNar, Peking* shes

****

Avoiding words which pertain to the essence, not reciting that which wounds mortally, one who speaks about the nature of others should do so like a person with a cutting instrument.

****

(1) cr 582, 583; CR 7.13; CS 2.7; MBh 12.138.24; GP 1.114.15.

(2) IS 3692

****

Cr 582 nātmacchidraṃ pare dadyāt paracchidrāṇi lakṣayet
gūhet kūrma ivāṅgāni prabhāvaṃ parīkṣayet

(a) MBh, IS nāsya chidraṃ paro vidyād; Cr 583, CS paro vidyād

(b) MBh, IS, Cr 583, CS vidyāc chidraṃ parasya tu; GP vidyāc chidraṃ parasya ca

(c) GP gṛhe

(d) MBh IS rakṣed vivaramātmanaḥ; Cr 583, CS, GP ca lakṣayet

****

2.3 sñin la tsham tshom med byas te
bu ram chu bzhin kha nas brjod
zhe 'gras yid ches byas nas ni
de nas ṅag gam mtshon gyis gzhom

1.7 *sNar, Peking* nas

4.1 *sNar* da

4.3 *dGe* dag

****

Without any hesitation in one's heart, one should speak aloud making it like a sugar juice mixture.

Having believed someone with a hateful heart, then one will become vanquished by weapons or speech.

****

No similar verses were found in Sanskrit.

2.4 dgra rnams sñan par brjod kyaṅ ni
blo ldan btaṅ sñoms mi byo
de ñid mthar ni gnod byed de
ji ltar dug snod mi bzad bzhin

1.4 *sDe, Cone* pa

2.4 *sNar* slobs

4.4 *sDe, Cone* gnod

4.6 *Peking* bzan

****

Wise men should not be apathetic toward enemies although they speak sweetly, since in the end such ones cause injury just as pots of poison do.

****

(1) Cr 978; CR 3.40; GP 110.20

****

Cr śatror apatyāni priyaṃvadāni nopekṣitavyāni buddhāir manusyāiḥ
tāny eṣu kāleṣu vipatakarāṇi viṣasya pātrāny api dāruṇāni

(a) CR vasaṃ gatāni

(b) CR nopekṣaṇīyāṇi

(c) CR Tanyeva kālena; GP tāny eva

(d) CR batāsipatrādapi dāruṇāni; GP hi

2.5 rān stobs chu bo mi brtan te
chu bo'i rgya knon yoṅs brtags nas
de bzhin dus su brgyal bya ste
raṅ gi don rnams rjes su bsam

3.6 *sNar, Peking* byas

3.7 *sNar, Peking* te

4.2 *sDe, Cone* don

4.3 *sDe, Cone* de

4.4 *sDe, Cone* bzhin

4.5 *sNar* rje

****

One's own force and the force of a river are not steadfast. Having contemplated the size of the river, then one who is desirous of crossing should consider his own welfare.

****

No similar verses were found in Sanskrit.

2.6 ji srid 'jigs pa ma byuṅ bar
de srid bar du 'jigs par bya
'jigs pa mṅon sum byuṅ na ni
'jigs pa btaṅ ste brdeg par bya

1.7 *sDe, Cone* ba

****

As long as danger does not appear, so long should one be on guard; when danger appears, having confronted the danger, one should attack.

****

(1) Cr 418; CV 5.3; CR 8.42; MBh 12.138.33; PP 1.170; HJ 1.58, 4.17; HP 4.17; HH 15.6-7; HK 1.57, 4.17; GP 1.115.45

(2) SV 2755; SP 1306; SRBh 266.520; IS 2550, 4593.

****

Cr tāvad bhayasya bhetavyaṃ yāvad bhayam anāgatam
āgatam tu bhayaṃ dṛṣṭva prahartavyam abhītavat

(a) CV bhayeṣu; CR, SRBh bhayād dhi; MBh, IS 4593 bhītavat saṃvidhātavyaṃ; HJ 4.17, HK 4.17, IS 2550 bhayāt tu.

(b) HP na bhayam āgatam

(c) HJ ca vīkṣya; HP, HH, HK 1.57, HK 4.17, SRBh vīkṣya

(d) CV aśaṅkayā; PP aśaṅkitāiḥ; HJ 1.58, HH, HK 1.57 naraḥ kuryād yathocitaṃ

2.7 don ni chu skyar bzhin du bsam
pha rol gnod pa seṅ ge bzhin
byi la'i dri tshor byi ba ltar
shes nas shin tu brtul bar bya

1.7 *sNar, Peking* bsam

2.3 *sDe, Cone* gnon

3.2 *sDe, Cone* ba'i

3.6 *sDe, Cone* la

4.2 *sNar, Peking* don

4.4 *sNar, Peking* du

****

Think of possessions as a water bird (does) and likewise consider an enemy who is troubling you as a lion would.

Just as a mouse who senses the smell of a cat, one who knows this will be diligent.

****

(1) Mbh 12.138.25

(2) IS 4378; SS Arthaparva 35.34

****

Mbh bakavac cintayed arthān siṃhavac ca parākramet
vṛkavac cāvâlumpeta śaśavac ca viniṣpatet

****

The Tibetan translators have completely misunderstood the Sanskrit. The Sanskrit reads: One should consider possessions as a crane does and one should approach things as a lion does; one should seize things as a wolf does and escape as a rabbit does.

2.8 seṅ ge'i gcig daṅ chu skyar gcig
bya gag gi ni bslam pa bzhi
bya rog lṅa daṅ khyi yi drug
bod bi'i kbslam pa gsum rnams so

1.3 *sNar, Peking* cig

1.7 *sNar, Peking* bzhi

4.6 *sNar* rnam

****

A lion has a single thing to teach, likewise a heron has one thing to teach, but a cock has four things, a raven has five things, a dog has six things, and a donkey has three things to teach.

****

(1) Cr 1076; CV 6.14; Cv 5.3; CN 64; CS 2.21

(2) SRBh 262.415; IS 7041

****

Cr siṃhād eaṃ bakād ekaṃ ṣaṭ śunas trīṇi gardabhāt
vāyasāt pañca śikṣc ca catvāri kukkuṭādapi

(b) CS, CV, Cv śikṣec catvāri kukkuṭāt

(d) CS, CV, Cv ṣaṭśunas trīṇi gardabhāt

2.9 bya ba maṅ ñuṅ gaṅ yaṅ ruṅ
skyes bu gaṅ zhig byed 'dod pa
rtog med bya ba kun brtsams te
seṅ ge'i gcig ces grags pa yin

3.6 *sDe, Cone* bsal

4.6 *sDe* ba

****

A man who desires to carry out his duty, whether large or small should commence the duty without a second thought; this single thing is a well known trait of a lion.

****

(1) Cr 691; CV 6.15; Cv 5.4; CS 2.22; CN 65

(2) SRBh 262.416, IS 4261

****

Cr 691 prabhūtaṃ kāryam alpaṃ vā yo naraḥ kartum icchati
sarvārambheṇa tat kuryāt simhād ekaṃ prakirtitam

(a) SRBh alpakāryam

(c) CS sarvārambheṣu tat karyam

(d) Cs vidhīyate; CV prackṣate

2.10 dbaṅ po rnams ni rab bsdams shiṅ
yul daṅ dus la ci rigs par
bya ba rnams ni brtag dpyod de
skeys bu mdzaṅs pa chu skyar bzhin

3.5 *sNar, Peking* rtag

3.6 *Peking* dpyad

****

A wise man, holding back his *indriyas* (senses) in the manner of a heron, examines things which are to be done in relation to what is proper for the time and place.

****

(1) Cr 1058; CV 6.16; Cv 5.5; CS 2.23; CN 66

(2) SRBh 262.417; IS 6950

****

Cr sarvendriyāṇi saṃyamya bakavat paṇḍito janaḥ
kāladeśopapannāni sarvakāryāṇi sādhyet

(a) CV, Cv indriyāṇi ca; CS indriyāṇi tu

(b) CV, Cv, CS, IS naraḥ

(c) CV, Cv deśakālabalam jñātvā; CS kāryakālopapannāti

2.11 tho raṅs ldaṅ daṅ 'thab pa daṅ
gñen la kha zas sñoms par 'gyed
mo la rab gnon ñe bar spyod
khyim bya'i bslab pa bzhi yin no

3.7 *Cone* stod

4.4 *sNar, Peking* ma

****

The four things to be learned from a cock are the getting up at dawn, disputing, making food equal among relatives, and performing the subduing of women.

****

(1) Cr 688; CV 6.17; Cv 5.6; CS 2.24; CN 70

(2) SRBh 262.421; IS 5510

****

Cr 688 pratyutthānaṃ ca yuddhaṃ ca saṃvibhāgaṃ ca bandhuṣu
striyam ākramya bhuñjīta śikṣec catvāri kukkuṭāt

(a) CS prāgutthanaṃ; CN, SRBh, IS yuddhaṃ ca prātarutthānaṃ

(b) CN, SRBh, IS bhojanaṃ saha bandhubhiḥ

(c) CN, SRBh, IS āpadgatāṃ rakṣec; CV, Cv svyam

(d) CN, SRBh catuḥ śikṣeta; IS catvāry etāni

2.12 mi mṅon 'khrig daṅ raṅam pa daṅ
dus su gnas ni 'cha'a ba daṅ
bag yod pa daṅ yid mi ches
'di ni bya rog bslab pa lṅa

1.5 *sDe, Cone* rnam

****

The five things to be learned from a raven are having sexual intercourse privately, being bold, constructing a nest at the proper time, being careful, and not being trusting.

****

(1) Cr 355; CV 6.18; Cv 5.7; CS 2.25; CN 69

(2) SRBh 262.420; IS 2183

****

CV gūḍhamāithunaṃ dhārṣṭyaṃ ca kāle kāle ca saṃgraham
apramattam aviśvāsaṃ pañca śikṣec ca vāyasāt

(a) Cr, Cv, CN, ŚRBh, IS Guḍhamāithunadhārṣṭyāṃ; CS gūḍhamāithunadhṛṣṭatvaṃ

(b) Cv, SRBh Cālyasaṃgraham; CS ca balisaṃgrahaḥ

(c) Cr, CN, SRBh, IS apramādam anālasyaṃ; Cv apramādam aviśvāsaṃ; CS apramādī suthūrtaṃ

(d) Cr, CN, SRBh, IS sikṣeta

2.13 mān du za daṅ cuṅ zad chog
legs par gñid log myur du sad
dpa'a la sñin ñe brtan pa ste
khyi yi spyod pa drug yin no

2..6 *sNar, Peking* bar

4.1 *sNar, Peking* khyi'i

4.2*sNar, Peking* spyod

4.3 *sNar, Peking* pa

4.4 *sNar, Peking* drug

4.5 *sNar, Peking* yin

4.6 *sNar, Peking* no

****

The six things done by a dog are desiring a great deal while being satisfied with only a little amount, falling asleep easily while awakening quickly, and being affectionate towards the master while being steadfast.

****

(1) Cr 714; CV 6.19; Cv 5.8; CS 2.26; CN 67

(2) SRBh 262.418; IS 4427

****

Cr bahvāśī svalpasaṃtuṣṭaḥ sunidraḥ śīghracetanaḥ
prabhubhaktaś ca sūraśca jñatavyā ṣaṭ śuno guṇāḥ

(a) Cv, CS cālpasaṃtuṣṭaḥ

(b) CV, Cv laghucetanaḥ

(c) Cv, Cv, CS svāmibhaktaś

(d) CV, Cv, CS ṣaḍete śvānato

2.14 khal gyis bkal na 'degs pa daṅ
graṅ daṅ tsha bas mi bskyod daṅ
rtag tu chog ni shes pa ste
boṅ bi'i kspyod pa gsum yin no

2.5 *sDe, Cone* skyo

4.4 *sNar* ba

****

The three things done by a donkey are carrying a load which had been loaded on, not being irritated by hot or cold, and knowing continual contentment.

****

(1) Cr 100; CV 6.20; Cv 5.9; CS 2.27; CN 68

(2) SRbh 262. 419; IS 694

****

Cr avišrāmaṃ vahed bhāraṃ śītoṣṇaṃ ca na vindati
sasaṃtoṣas tathā nityaṃ trīṇi śikṣeta gardabhāt

(a) CV suśrānto 'pi; CS aviśrāntam

(b) CV na ca paśyati; Cv na ca

(c) CV saṃtuṣṭaścareta; Cv susaṃtuṣṭaḥ sadā; CS susaṃtuṣṭo baven

(d) CV, Cv śikṣec ca

2.15 sw ltar ñi shu shes bya ste
skyes bu gan zhig spyod 'gyur ba
'di ni dgra las rgyal 'gyur te
dgra rnams kun gyis tshugs mi 'gyur

1.4 *sNar, Peking* shur

4.5 *sNar, Peking* mi

4.6 *sNar, Peking* rhub

****

Whatever man thus practicing these twenty activities will become victorious over enemies and will not be defeated by any enemies.

****

(1) Cr 220, 792; CV 6.21; Cv 5.10; CS 2.28

****

CS viṃsatyete gunāḥ proktā yastu kuryād vickṣamaḥ
sa jeṣyati ripūn sarvān jeyaś ca na bhaviṣyati

(a) Cr 220, Cv etāni viṃsatipadāny; Cr 792, CV ya etān viṃsatiguṇān
(b) Cr 220, Cv ācariṣyati yo naraḥ; Cr 792, CV ācariṣyati mānavaḥ
(c) Cr 792, Cv kāryavasthāsu sarvāsu
(d) Cr 220, Cv kalyāṇaś ca; Cr 792, CV ajeyaḥ sa

3.1 ji srid dus la ma bab par
dgra ni phrag goṅ bkur bya ste
de bzhin dus su phyin gyur na
rdo la rdza ma bsnun bzhin gzhom

****

One should carry any enemy on one's shoulder until the proper time has arrived. When the proper time has arrived, one should vanquish him like a pot a stone.

****

(1) Cr 921; CS 2.10; Cr 5.28; MBh 12.138.18; Pp 3.213; PRE 3.93; PS 3.66; PT 3.94; PTK 3.107; HJ 4.65; HP 4.65; HM 4.61; HH 109.19-20; HS 4.60; HK 4.66
(1) SV 2754; SRK 266.31; SRBh 250.91; IS 6013; SS Arthaparva 35.36

****

Cr vahed amitraṃ skandhena yāvat kālaviparyayaḥ
athāivam āgate kāle bhindyād ghaṭam ivāśamni

(a) PP, PRE, PS, PT, PTK, CR skandenāpi vahecchatruṃ; HJ, HP, HM, HH, HS, HK skandenāpi vahecchatrūn
(b) SV, IS kālasya paryayaḥ; PP, PS PT kālamāsādya buddhimān PRE, PTK, HJ, HP, HM, HH, HS, HK kāryamāsādya buddhimān; CS kālam vivarjayet
(c) CS tathāivam; CR tam eva kāle saṃprāpte; IS prāptakalaṃ tu vijñāya; PP, PS, PT mahatā kṛṣṇasarpeṇa; Pre, PTK vahatā kṛṣṇasarpeṇa; HJ, HP, HM, HH, HS, HK yatha vṛddhena sarpeṇa
(d) PP amṇḍūkā bahavo hatāḥ; PRE, PTK, PS, PT, HJ, HP, HM, HH, HK, HS maṇḍūkā vinipātitāḥ

****

The *Pañcatantra* and *Hitopadśa* versions do not use upamā of the pot breaking on the stone but refer to the story of the frog and the old snake.

****

3.2 dman bzhiṅ sñiṅ rje'i skad brjod kyaṅ
dgra ni gtaṅ bar mi bya'o
de la sñin rje mi bya zhiṅ
sṅon chad gnod pa byed pa gzhom

1.2 *sDe, Cone* zhin

1.6 *sNar, Peking* 'don

2.3 *sNar, Peking* braṅ

****

One should not let an enemy escape even if he speaks in a pitiful voice as an inferior person; one should not show pity to such a one and should conquer those who have caused harm in the past.

****

(1) MBh 12.138.52; PT 3.64; PTK 3.75

(2) IS 520; SS ARthaparva 113.25

****

MBh amitraṃ nāiva muñceta bruvantaṃ karuṇāny api
duḥkhaṃ tatra na kurv*Ibid*.,ta hanyāt purvapakāriṇam

(a) PT, PTK vimuñcet

(b) PT, PTK bruvāṇaṃ; IS vadantaṃ

(c) PT, PTK, IS kartavyaṃ

3.3 bu lon me yi lhag ma daṅ
de bzhin dgra yi lhag ma ni
yaṅ daṅ yaṅ du 'phel 'gyur bas
de bas lhag ma gzhag mi vya

4.5 *sNar, Peking* bzhag

****

The remains of a debt and a fire are like the remains of an enemy; they will become spread again and again and thus one should not leave behind any remainder of these things.

****

(1) Cr 194; CS 3.58; CR 8.45; GP 1.115.46; MBh 12.138.58; PP 3.219; PRE 3.99; PS 3.69; PKB 3.178; CN 38
(2) SV 2760 ; SP 1491; IS 1332; SS Arthaparva 35.48

****

Cr ṛṇśeṣo 'gniśeṣaś ca śatruśeṣas tathāiva ca
punaḥ punaḥ pravardhante tasmān niḥśeṣam ācaret

(a) PRE, PP, IS ṛṇaśeṣamagniśeṣaṃ; GP, PS, PKB ṛṇaśeṣaṃ cāgniśeṣam
(b) PP, PKB, IS śatruśeṣaṃ; PRE, PS, GP vyādhiśeṣaṃ; CS vyādhiśeṣas
(c) MBh punarvivardheta; CR, SP pravartante; CS punaś ca vardhate yasmāt; PP vyādhiśeṣam ca niḥśeṣaṃ; SS also 'pi vardhate `tyarthaṃ; PRE, PS ariśeṣam ca nihśeṣam
(d) GS, GP, SP tasmāc cheṣaṃ na kārayet; MBh svalpo 'py anivāritaḥ; PP, PS PRE kṛtvā prājño na sīdati; PKB, IS tasmāc cheṣaṃ na dhārayet; SS tac cheṣaṃ nāiva kārayet

3.4 byas la lan du phan bya ste
'chi ba byed la slar yaṅ gtse
de la ñes par mi lta zhiṅ
ma ruṅs byed la ma ruṅs bya

1.1 *sNar, Peking* byams

2.2 *sNar, Peking* bar

2.4 *Peking* pa

3.3 *sNar, Peking* nes

3.6 *sNar, Peking* blta

4.2 *sDe, Cone* run

4.2 *sDe, Cone* su

4.2*sDe, Cone* byed

4.3 *sDe, Cone* lam

4.7 *sNar, Peking* sbyad

****

One should return a favour when it is needed and one should cause harm in return to those who produce harm. There is no seeing fault when one is deceitful to those who are deceitful.

****

(1) Cr 296; CV 17.2; GP 1.115.47; Pp 5.64; PKB 5.84

(2) SRBh 268.569; IS 1874

****

Cr kṛte pratikṛtaṃ kuryād dhiṃsite pratihiṃsitam
tatra doṣaṃ na paśyāmi yo duṣṭe duṣṭam ācaret

(b) CV hiṃsane pratihiṃsanam

(c) PP, PKB, SRBh, GP na tatra doṣaṃ; CV tatra doṣo na patati

(d) PKB, SRBh, CV duṣṭ duṣṭam samācret; GP duṣṭe doṣam samācaret

****

The Sanskrit reads: One should do good deeds to one who does good deeds and one should cause injury to those who injure. I do not see the fault in the case where one acts wickedly towards a wicked person.

3.5 phoṅs pa'i don du nor rnams bsruṅ
nor bas chuṅ ma bsruṅ bar bya
nor daṅ chuṅ ma gñis bas kyaṅ
thams cad don du bdag bsruṅ ṅo

1.1 *sNar, Peking* 'phans

****

One should guard wealth against the time of poverty; one should protect one's wives with wealth; (but) one should protect one's self at all times even at the cost of one's wealth and one's wives.

****

(1) Cr 142; CV 1.6; Cv 1.6; CN k27; CR 2.1; GP 1.109.1; MBh 5.37.17; PKB 1.356 and 3.86; HJ 1.43; ;HP 1.31; HM 1.41; HH 12.15-16; HS 1.36; HK 1.42
(2) SRBh 260.366; IS 958

****

Cr āpadarthe dhanaṃ rakṣed dārān rakṣed dhanāir api
ātmānam satataṃ rakṣed dārāir api dhanāir api

(a) CN, CR, SRBh, IS, MBh, HP, HK āpadarthaṃ; CR rakṣyam

(c) cr ātmā tu sarvato rakṣyo; Cv sa taṃ

3.6 lkog na 'phya ba ñams byed ciṅ
mṅon sum snan par smra byed pa
de 'dra'i grogs bo spaṅ bya ste
bum kha'i 'o ma bzhin no

1.3 *sNar, Peking* bya

1.5 *sDe, Cone* byams

4.2 *sNar, Peking* pa'i

4.4 *sDe, Cone* ma'i

4.6 *sNar* bzhi

****

In secret making vile abuse while in public he has sweet speech; such a friend as this should be abandoned like a jar of poison which has milk on top.

****

(1) Cr 646; CV 2.5; Cv 2.5; CN 16; CS 3.61; CR 8.49; GP 1.115.48; PP 1.284; HJ 1.78; HH 18.19-20; HS 1.71; HK 1.78
(2) SRBh 131.1; IS 3979; SRK 63.2

****

Cr parokṣe kāryahantāraṃ pratyakṣ priyavādinam
varjayet tādṛśaṃ mitraṃ viṣakumbhaṃ payomukham

(a) PP guṇahantāraṃ

(b) CR kuṭilaṃ

(d) GP māyāmayamarin tathā

****

The Tibetan translators seem to have read *garhayantāraṃ* rather than *kāryahantāraṃ*.

3.7 brkam chags sbyin pa mi ster daṅ
khenṅs thal mo mi sbyor daṅ
de dra'i glen pa'i rjes mthun par
ji ltar de ltar shes pa mkhas

4.2 *sDe, Cone* lta

4.5*sDe, Cone* thabs

4.6 *sDe, Cone* la

****

A person gives a gift to a greedy person; a person joins his palms before a proud person; likewise one complies with the wishes of a fool; (one offers) a wise man that which is as it is.

****

(1) Cr 890; CV 6.11; Cv 6.1; CN 31; Cr 2.16; GP 1.109.10; PS 1.26; Hj 4.108; HP 4.107; HM 4.104; HH 116.18-19; HS 4.102; HK 4.109

(2) SRBh 250.99; IS 5860, SS ARthaparva 35.85

****

Cr lubdham arthena gṛhṇīyāt stabdham añjalikarmaṅā
mūrkhaṃ chandānuvṛttena yathārthena ca paṇḍitam

(a) CR, Gp arthapradānena

(b) CN, SRBh, IS kruddham; GP ślaghyam

(c) CV, Cv, CN, HM, HH, HS, IS chando 'nuvṛ5ttena; PS, GP, SRBh chandānuvṛttyā; HK, SS chandānurodhena

(d) Cv, CN, GP, PS, HP, HH, HM, HS, HK, SS tathyena; IS tathā tathyena CR vaśīkurvanti pandWitāḥ

****

The Tibetan translators have misunderstood the Sanskrit. They have changed the meaning of the verse. The Sanskrit reads; One should conciliate a greedy person with a gift, a proud man with an *añjali*, a fool by complying with his desires, and a wise man with whatever is appropriate. In addition, the Tibetan verse makes use of the word for person without the noun indicator *pa*.

3.8 dgra la thal sbyar yid ches daṅ
spyi bos gtugs te gus bya zhiṅ
gduṅ gyur mchi ma 'dzag sogs bya
'byor par 'dod pas de ltar spyad

2.3 *sNar, Peking* btud

4.7 *sNar, Peking* bya

****

One who desires to thrive should act as follows: he should inspire trust by making *añjalis* to enemies, he should be respectful by bowing the head, and he should shed tears of affliction.

****

(1) MBh 12.138.17

(2) IS 117, MSS 469

****

MBh añjaliṃ śapathaṃ sāntvaṃ praṇamya śirasā vadet
aśruprapātanam cāiva kartavyaṃ bhūtim icchatā

(a) IS Añjaliḥ śapathaḥ

(c) IS aśrupramārjanaṃ

****

The Tibetan translators have misunderstood *śapatham* as *sapatnam*.

3.9 dgra bo stobs ldan rjes mthun bya
stobs chuṅ dgra bo brlag bya ste
mthu stobs mñnam pa'i dgra la ni
mthun min gdul la min bya ba'o

2.4 *sNar, Peking* la

2.5 *sNar, Peking* klag

4.3 *sDe du; Cone* dul

****

Make a treaty with an enemy who possesses great power; demolish an enemy who has little strength; concerning an enemy who has equal strength, there is no treaty and no conquering.

****

(1) Cr 59; Cv 6.2; CV 7.10

(2) IS 324, MSS 1507

****

Cr anulomena balinaṃ pratilomean durjanam
ātmatulyabalaṃ śatruṃ vinayena balena vā

(b) Cv durbalaṃ

(c) Cv samatulyabalaṃ

(d) Cv ca

****

The Tibetan seems too have read *na jayena* for *vinayana*.

3.10 gaṅ gis gduṅ 'gyur de mi bya
gaṅ gis zhum 'gyur tshul mi spyad
mthar mi phyin pa'i las mi brtsam
mgo ltuṅ mi 'gyur gdeg mi bya

2.5 *sNar, Peking* de

4.5 *sDe, Cone* brdeg

****

One should not do that which causes torment; one should not do that which causes dismay; one should not begin that work which cannot be finished; so that one's head does not fall one should not stick one's neck out.

****

No similar verses were found in Sanskrit.

3.11 pha rol ma brgal de mi brtsad
gaṅ du dgra rnams der 'dug min
shiṅ rtsa ma phyuṅ phyuṅ ba min
gñis su ma gyur bcad pa min

1.3 *sDe, Cone* mi

1.4 *sDe, Cone* rgal

1.7 *sNar, Peking* brtsam

2.4 *sNar, Peking* gnas

****

There should be no quarreling or arguing with enemies; there is no residence where there are enemies; a tree root that is not removed does not remove anything else; there is no cutting that which is single.

****

No similar verses were found in Sanskrit.

3.12 rgan po med pa'i tshogs pa min
chos mi ston gaṅ rgan pa min
gaṅ la bden med chos ma yin
tshig don ma 'brel don ma yin

1.4 *sDe, Cone* pa

1.5 *sNar, Peking* 'tshogs

2.4 *sNar, Peking* dag

3.6 *sNar, Peking* kyaṅ

3.7 *sNar, Peking* med

4.3 *sNar, Peking* 'brel

4.4 *sNar, Peking* med

****

There is no assembly where there are no elders: they are not elders who do not speak the *dharma*; there is no *dharma* where there is no truth; that which is mixed with deception is not the truth.

****

(1) Cr 570; Cr k8.53; MBh 5.35.49; GP 1.115.52; HJ 3.64; HP 3.59; HM 3.61; HH 84.16-17; HS 3.61; HK 3.61
(2) SP 1344; SRBh 284.945; IS 3483; SS Arthaparva 135.68

****

Cr na sa sabhā yatra na santi vṛddhā
vṛddhā na te ye na vadanti dharmam
dharmaḥ sa no yatra na satyam asti
satyaṃ na tad yac chaladoṣayuktam

(b) MBh, SS na te vṛddhā
(c) SS, MBh, IS, SS nāsāu dharmo; SARBh dharmo na vāi yatra ca nāsti satyaṃ; CR asti satyaṃ

3.13 tsher ma gtiṅ du zug pa daṅ
chos las ñams pa ñ id dañ ni
dgra daṅ sha khon zhugs pa ni
rtsa nas phyuṅ ba bde ba yin

1.5 *sDE* zugs; *Cone* gzugs

2.2 *sNar, Peking* la

3.4 *sNar, Peking* 'khon

3.7 *sDe, Cone* gsum

4.1 *sNar, Peking* rtsad

4.4 *sNar, Peking* na

****

Happiness is the pulling up from the root of a thorn that is embedded, of a person who has fallen from the *dharma*, and of an enemy who is hostile.

****

(1) Cr 228; CR 8.71; PP 1.222; PRE 1.67; PS 1.59; PTK 1.65; HJ 2.127; HP 2.115; HM 2.129; HH 63.5-6; HS 2.122; HK 2.127
(2) SRBh 237.216; IS 1506; SV 2805

****

Cr kaṇṭ akasya vimagnasya dantasya calitasya ca
amātyasyā ċa duṣṭasya mulā duddharaṇaṃ sukham

(a) PP ca magnasya; PTK tu magnasya; PS viṣadigdhasya bhakṣyasya; PRE, HJ, HM, HK, SRBh viṣadigdhasya bhaktasya; HP vidagdhasya ca bhuktasya; HH viraktasya ca bhaktasya; HS vidagdasya ca bhaktasya
(b) HH galitasya
(d) PS balād; HS uddharaṇāt; HH, SV, IS varam

****

The examples used in the Tibetan are not the same as in the Sanskrit verses cited. The Sanskrit reads: It is by pulling it up the root that one gets ease from an embedded thorn, a loose tooth, and a treacherous minister.

3.14 gtan du draṅ po mi bya ste
ngas su soṅ la yoṅs ltos daṅ
der ni shiṅ daṅ gcod 'gyur te
yon pa'i shiṅ ni gnas la ltos

4.2 *sNar, Peking* po'i

****

One should not always be upright; go and observe what takes place in the forest where the perfectly straight trees are cut down and the crooked ones remain.

****

(1) Cr 584; CG 7.12; Cv 6.5, CR 7.46; GP 1.114.50

(2) SV 2758; IS 3564

****

Cr nātyantasaralāir bhāvyaṃ gatvā paśya vanasthalīm
chidyante saralās tatra kubjās tiṣṭhanti pādapāḥ

(a) CV, Cv, GP atyantaṃ

(b) SV vane tarūn; GP Nātyantaṃ mṛdunātathā

(c) GP, Cv saralās tatra chidyante

(d) SV, CR kubjaḥ santi pade pade

3.15 gaṅ daṅ gaṅ ni ci bsams pa
de daṅ de la phan bsams te
rjes su 'jug pa'i mkhas pa ni
myur du bdag gi bdaṅ du 'gyur

1.4 *sNar, Peking* la

1.5 *sNar, Peking* bsam

****

When one is going to think about something for someone, he should think about that which is beneficial for himself. Learned men who practice this will quickly gain power over themselves.

****

No similar verses were found in Sanskrit.

3.16 'di ltar gsad bya gaṅ yin pa
mi brjod ma tshor gsad bya ste
ri dgas rgyal po rab 'khrugs pas
lus bskums na ni gsod byed bzhin
sñiṅ la khon du dam bzuṅ nas
gzhan la ma ston spyad pas bya
blo ldan bzod ba ldan byas nas
bzhan gyi skyon ni yoṅ mi bgraṅ

1.7 *sDe, Cone* de

4.3 *sNar, Peking* nas

4.5 *sDe, Cone* gnod

4.7 *sDe, Cone* bzhin

6.3 *sNar, Peking* mi

6.4 *sDe, Cone* ltos

7.4 *sDe, Cone* daṅ

8.5 *sDe, Cone* yaṅ

****

Whoever would kill without being heard should act in the manner of a lion who crouches before he kills. Holding anger in their hearts wise men do not show it to others and do not take account of the affronts of others but put up with them for the time being.

****

(1) PP 3.35; PKB 3.43

(2) SV 2935; IS 5179; SS Arthaparva 65.13

PP yad apasarati meṣaḥ kāraṇaṃ tat prahartum
mṛgapatir atikopāt samkucaty utpatiṣṇuḥ
hṛdayanihitavāirā gūḍhamantrapracārāḥ
kimapi vigaṇayanto buddhimantaḥ sahante

(b) IS api kopāt; SS api roṣāt...utpatipyan

(c) PKB hṛdayanihitabhāvā

(d) SV, SS kṣamante; SS kim iva hi

****

The Sanskrit reads: A ram moves backward in order to attack; the king of beasts crouches when about to spring in anger, the wise hide their enmity and use secret means disregarding (affronts) and putting up with them for a while.

3.17 dper na khu byug grog ma daṅ
dṅul rdo lta bu'i mdog ldan pa'i
lag 'gro'i rkaṅ mthil gaṅ yin des
dus ma yin par ñams kyaṅ ni

gaṅ zhig blo gros la brten te
gdeṅs ka go 'phaṅ mi smad ciṅ
de ni dug ñams mi 'gyur ltar
skyes bu ñams kyaṅ go 'phaṅ mtho

3.7 *sNar, Peking* de

5.6 *sNar, Peking* bsten

6.4 *sNar, Peking* 'phaṅs

8.2 *sNar, Peking* bus

****

For example, cuckoos, ants, and the underside of a snake all possess the color of iron ore, but they are hurt when they are out of season. Whoever depends upon wisdom with his head upright will not be hurt, just so, although one is sometimes hurt, one's dignity will be maintained.

****

No similar verses were found in Sanskrit.

3.18 ji srid dgra bo pha rol la
'dir ni pus btsugs gduñ bya ste
skye bo dam pa rnams la ni
bsñen bkur sna tshog spyod pa dan
rṅon ba'i spyod lam 'jab bu yis
ri dgas druṅ du phyin nas ni
dug bsgos mda'a yis bsnun bzhin bya

1.1 *sDe, Cone* ci

2.1 *sNar, Peking* 'dis

3.5 *sNar* rnam

5.1 *sDe, Cone* rdon

5.5 *sNar, Peking* 'jam

6.5 *sNar, Peking* bsñen

****

To a foreign enemy show reverence and pay various offerings as one would to a holy person; one should follow the sneaky manner of a hunter, who having come to the vicinity of a beast, then pierces it with a poison-smeared arrow.

****

No similar verses were found in Sanskrit.

4.1 bdag don 'bad bas bya ba ste
gzhan don dẹ bzhin bsam mi bya
bdag gzhan don rnams spaṅs pas ni
mdzaṅs pa thob par mi 'gyur ro

3.6 *sNar, Peking* pa

****

One should engage in one's own *artha* and should not pay attention to the *artha* of others. By abandoning one's own *artha* and the *artha* of others, one does not become wise.

****

(2) MSS 4662

****

MSS ātmārtham yuktavittānāṃ mitramaṇḍalabhedīnām
atliañghitalokānāṃ na bandhaḥ kenacit kvacit

The Sanskrit does not mention wisdom.

4.2 gzhan gyi don la mi brtul te
raṅ gi las la brtson par bya

2.5 *sDe* brtsan

2.6 *sDe, Cone* pas

****

Not acting in regard to the *artha* of others, one should strive in regards to the deeds of one's own.

****

No similar verses were found in Sanskrit. MBh 5.33.31 contains the same essential idea but the text is sufficiently different so that it could not be considered the root verse of the above verse.

svamarthaṃ yaḥ parityajya parārtham anutiṣṭhati
mithyācarati mitrārthe yaś ca muḍhah sa ucyate

4.3 mig sman spyad na zad snaṅ zhiṅ
grog ma yis ni bsags pa daṅ
de bzhin du ni mkhas pa yis
bsags pa ñud du spyad par bya

1.5 *sNar, Peking* brad

2.3 *sNar* yid

2.7 *sNar, Peking* ltar

****

Having seen the wearing off of colyrium and the accumulation of an anthill, a wise man accordingly prepares his accumulation little by little.

****

Lines 1 and 2 of this verse have several Sanskrit occurrences but lines 3 and 4 were not found in any Sanskrit verses.

Pādas a and b of the following correspond to lines 1 and 2 above:

(1) Cr 15; CR 5.39; Cv 6.15; GP 1.113.8; HJ 2.9; HP 2.10; HM 2.12: HH 4.113-14; HS 2.9; HK 2.10

(2) SP 650; SV 2684; SRBh 248.43; IS 115; SS Dharmaparva 7.1

****

Cr (ab) añjanasya kṣayaṃ dṛṣṭvā valmīkasya ca saṃcayam

(b) GP, HS, HH, SP, SRBh tu; SS vardhanam

4.4 ma rmoṅs thams cad rmoṅs bya zhiṅ
rmoṅs rnams rtag tu mgo bskor bya
yid mi ches la yid ches bya
bdag ñid sba zhiṅ rjes su bsam

4.5 *sDe, Cone* gzhan

4.6 *sDe, Cone* rjes

****

Cunning men will delude everybody; fools will always be cheated; some will believe in those who are untrustworthy; consider the concealed nature (of people).

****

No similar verses were found in Sanskrit.

4.5 ñi ma don med mi bya ste
spyin pa kha ton las rnams bya
ji ltar srin byi kha chu yis
grog ma bslus ba bzhin du bya

2.7 *sNar, Peking* spyad

3.4 *sDe, Cone* 'od

4.1 *Peking* grogs

****

One should perform deeds of giving and reciting which will cause the day to be profitable. Similarly one should act like the ant who decoys the worm with his spittle.

****

Lines 1 and 2 occur in several Sanskrit verses but lines 3 and 4 were not found in any Sanskrit verses. Pādas ca and d of the following verses correspond to lines 1 and 2 above:

(1) Cr 15, 1009; CV 2.13; Cv 2.16, 6.15; CR 5.39; GP 1.113.8; HJ 2.9; HP 2.10; HM 2.12; HH 41.13-14; HS 2.9; HK 2.10
(2) SP 650; SV 2684; SRBh 248.43; IS 115, 6594; SS Dharmaparva 71.

****

Cr 1009 avandhyaṃ divasaṃ kuryād dānādhyayanakarmabhiḥ
(c) Cr 15, CV, Cv 6.15, HM, HH, HS abandhyaṃ
(d) Cv 2.16 yadīcchetsubhamātmanaḥ; GP, HP, HM, HH, HS, HK, SRBh dānādhyayanakarmasu

4.6 dam pa'i skye bo dga'a bar bya
mi bsrun skye po bsten mi bya
skye bo ma ruṅs yid mi brtan
skye bo dgra la dpa'a brtan bya
bla ma'i skye bo bzod par bya
smad 'tshoṅ ma ni brid par bya

2.2 *sDe, Cone* srun

4.6 *sNar, Peking* ba

4.7 *sNar, Peking* brtan

6.4 *sNar, Peking* la

****

One should make virtuous people happy; one should not attend upon undisciplined people; one should not trust deceitful men; a person who is steadfast against enemies should be depended upon; holy men should be honored; one should cheat prostitutes.

****

No similar verses were found in Sanskrit.

4.7 gaṅ gis de dag ma lus par
thams cad yoṅs su shes gyur pa
des ni blaṅ dor dpyad pa yis
'jig rten 'jig rten shes pa yin

sNar, Peking line 3 does not appear in these texts.

****

Whoever would come to know two categories completely would know the transitory world as transitory; these two categories are things which should be kept and things which should be shunned.

****

No similar verses were found in Sanskrit.*

4.8 gaṅ daṅ gaṅ la nor ldan pa'i
skyes bu las la chags 'gyur ba
gaṅ daṅ gaṅ la dga'a ba'i tshig
de daṅ de yi yon tan brzod

1.5 *sNar, Peking* don

2.6 *sNar, Peking* gyur

****

In whatever result that comes from an action performed by a wealthy man and in whatever result there is in a word from a happy man, there is merit.

****

No similar verses were found in Sanskrit.

4.9 yid mi ches la yid mi brtan
yid ches lhag par yid brtan min
yid ches pa las 'jigs pa 'byuṅ
rtsa ba las kyaṅ gcod par byed

1.7 *sDe, Cone* brten

****

Do not ırust someone who is untrustworthy and do not be overly trusting of someone who is trustworthy. Danger that has arisen from trust cuts one off at the root.

****

(1) Cr 566; CR 7.42; CS 3.47; MBh 5.38.9, 12.136.138; GP 1.114.47; PP 4.12; PKB 2.39, 4.13
(2) sv 2734; is 3433

****

Cr na viśvased aviśvaste viśvaste nātiviśvaset
viśvāsād bhayamn utpannaṃ mūlānyapi nikṛntati

(a) GP aviśvastaṃ;

(b) PP, PKB 2.39, PKB 4.13, MBh 12.136.138 api na viśvaset

(d) GP, PP mūlād

4.10 'byuṅ po kun la yid mi brtan
kun la yid ches bya ba'aṅ min
raṅ gi raṅ bzhin sba bya zhin
gzhan gyi raṅ bzhin shes par gyis

3.1 *sDe, Cone* gan

4.2 *sNar, Peking* gyis

****

One should not rely on all creatures; one should never believe in everyone; one should conceal one's own nature; one should know the nature of others.

****

No similar verses were found in Sanskrit.

4.11 gzhan gyi bud med dug yin te
de bzhin chuṅ ma gzhan 'gro daṅ
gñis po de la yid rton pa'i
mi rnams 'chi sgor bsñen pa yin

4.5 *sNar, Peking* brten

****

The wife of another man is poison; likewise the wife who goes to another man (is poison); men who rely on either of these two women approach the door of death.

****

No similar verses were found in Sanskrit.

4.12 bud med rgyal po sbrul rnams daṅ
kha don dag daṅ dgra rnams daṅ
tshe daṅ loṅs spyod dag la ni
shes ldan rnams kyis yid brtan min

****

Wise men do not trust women, kings, snakes, loud recitations (of scripture), enemies, life, and enjoyments.

****

(1) Cr 2077; MBh 5.37.53; GP 1.114.46

(2) IS 7217

****

MBh strīṣu rājasu sarpeṣu svādhyaye śatruseviṣu
bhoge cāyasi viśvāsam kaḥ prājñaḥ kartum arhati

(a) Cr. GP rājāgnisarpeṣu

(b) Cr, GP śatrusevane; IS svādhyāyaprabhuśatruṣu

(c) Cr, GP bhogāsvādeṣu; ;IS bhogeṣv, viśvāsaḥ

4.13 rig pa 'dod pas mkhas brten bya
shes par gyur pa gzhan ston byed
de bas las rnams thams can ni
lus pa med par bslab par bya

2.4 *sNar, Peking* na

2.6 *sDe, Cone, Peking* sten

37 *sNar, Peking* daṅ

****

One who is desirous of knowledge should depend on a wiseman; when one has become learned, he teaches others; thus all actions will be taught completely.

****

No similar verses were found in Sanskrit.

4.14 sdig pa can la yid mi brtan
blo ldan bdag ces zer ches min
gan phyir de la yid ches min
de yi 'tsho ba ñams par 'gyur

3.4 *sNar, Peking* las

****

Do not rely upon one who possesses evil or one who says "I am learned;" one should not rely on such ones for any reason; the lives of such ones become polluted.

****

No similar verses were found in Sanskrit.

4.15 gshin rje'i gshed ma 'chi ba daṅ
sa 'og rgya mtsho'i gliṅ rnams daṅ
spu gri'i so dug sbrul dag ni
mi bsten phyogs gcig bud med yin

1.2 *sDe, Cone* rje

1.4 *sDe, Cone* po

2.4 *sDe, Cone* mtsho

3.2 *sDe, Cone* yi

3.6 *sNar, Peking* rnams

4.2 *sNar, Peking* ste

****

An undependable woman is at all times Yama's executioner, death itself, an island in the ocean of hell, and the poison of a razor and a snake.

****

(1) MBh 13.40.4

****

MBh agnir hi pramadā dipto māyāśca mayajā vibho
kṣuradhārā viṣaṃ sarpo mṛdtyur ity ekataḥ striyaḥ

****

The Sanskrit reads: All together a woman is a blazing fire; she is the deceptions of the goddess Maya; she is the edge of a razor; she is poison; she is a serpent; she is death itself.

4.16 dgra yi phyogs byed kspaṅ bar bya
bdag la dga'a ba yoṅs su bsdu
kun la blo ni yod pa ste
yun riṅ blo ni dga'a ba yin

4.5 *sDe, Cone* dka'a

****

One should abandon any action which causes benefit to an enemy; thus one will gather happiness for one's self; being wise in all matters, one is happy for along period of time.

****

No similar verses were found in Sanskrit.

4.17 mig 'byed mig 'dums tsam yaṅ ruṅ
dgra la mṅon sum bya ba min
smod pa na yaṅ 'on pa bzhin
dus bab ral gris bcad bzhin bya

1.4 *sNar, Peking* btsums

3.1 *sNar, Peking* dmod

3.3 *sNar, Peking* byas

3.4 *sNar, Peking* na

****

One should be blind to enemies as one is at the opening or closing of the eyes and one should be deaf to slander; at the appropriate time one should act as if one were cutting with a ritual sword.

****

(1) MBh 12.138.27 cd and MBh 12.138.28 ab

(2) IS 360 ab only

****

MBH andhaḥ syād andhvelāyām bādhiryam api saṃśrayet
deśaṃ kālaṃ samāsādya vikrameta vicakṣanaḥ

(b) cāśrayet

****

The Sanskrit reads: One should be blind when blindness is appropriate; one should also resort to deafness (when appropriate); at the proper time and place, the wise man makes his move.

4.18 gaṅ du chu yod ṅaṅ pa gnas
chu skams mtsho ni 'dor bar 'gyur
chu yis gaṅ na slar gnas bzhin
ṅaṅ pa lta bu'i grogs mi brtan

2.5 *sNar, Peking* skams

3.5 *sDe, Cone* phyir

4.7 *sNar, Peking* brten

****

One should not depend on a friend who is like a *haṃsa* (goose), since *haṃsas* establish themselves where there is water but when water dries up they depart and they settle again at a place where there is water.

****

(1) Cr 801; CV 7.13; Cv 6.6; CR 4.15

(2) IS 5085

****

CR yatrodakaṃ tatra caranti haṃsās tad eva śuṣkaṃ parivarjayanti prāpte jale tat punar āśrayante na haṃsamitrena nareṇa bhāvyam

(b) Cr CV, Cv tathāiva

(c) Cr, CV na haṃsatulyena nareṇa bhāvyam; Cv purnaṃ saras tat punar āśrayanti

(d) Cr, CV punas tyajante punar āśrayante; Cv na haṃsatulyena nareṇa bhāvyam

4.19 rgyal bo smad 'tshoṅ ma daṅ ni
de bzhin ñe du dman pa daṅ
gyog 'khor rnams la rtag tu yaṅ
ha caṅ gduṅ par mi bya'o

2.5 *sNar, Peking* sman

****

One should never be envious of a king, a prostitute, relatives, vile people, or servants.

****

(1) MBh 5.37.28

****

MBh ghṛṇī rājā pumscalī rāabhṛtyah putro bhrātā vidhavā bālaputrā
senājīvī coddhṛtabhakta eva vyavahāre vāi varjanīyāḥ
syur ete

****

The Sanskrit reads: One should avoid a lawsuit with a man of compassion, a king, a prostitute, a king's servants, a son, a brother, a widow with small sons, a soldier or someone who has loyal supporters.

4.20 gaṅgi rgyu las mya ṅan daṅ
dṅos daṅ sdug bsṅal ñid daṅ ni
lus kyi gnod byed rtsa ba de
gcig gam cuṅ zad tsam yaṅ ruṅ
mkhas phas spaṅ zhiṅ dor bas bya

2.1 *sDe, Cone* dar

3.2 *Peking* kyis

3.4 *sNar, Peking* bskyed

5.2 *Cone* pas

5.3 *sNar* spaṅs

****

A wise person having abandoned suffering from whatever cause, material possessions, pain itself, and that which at its root produces harm to the body should reject them one and all however many.

****

No similar verses were found in Sanskrit.

4.21 gser ni rnam bzhis brtag bya ste
bdar bcad bsreg daṅ brduṅ bar bya
de dzhin rnam bzhis skyes bu brtag
thos daṅ tshul khrims righ sñiṇ brtse

1.6 *sNar, Peking* pa

2.1 *sNar, Peking* brdar

2.6 *sNar, Peking* pas

2.7 *sNar, Peking* so

4.6 *sDe, Cone* la

4.7 *sDe, Cone* sogs

****

Just as gold should be examined for acceptability by grinding, cutting, burning, and smashing, just so a man should be examined for acceptability by listening, morality, family, and good nature.

****

(1) Cr 805; CV 5.2; Cv 4.6; CR 5.2; MBh 12.314.43; GP 1.112.3

(2) SRBh 286.980; SRK 276.26; IS 5104

****

CR yathā caturbhiḥ kanakaṃ parīkṣyate
nigharṣan acchedanatāpatāḍanāiḥ
tathā caturbhiḥ puruṣaḥ parīkṣyate
śrutenaśīlena kulena karmaṇā

(d) CV, IS tyāgena, guṇena; CR kulena, guṇena

4.22 thams cad shes shiṅ rig par bya
kun la dogs bya dus shes kyis
'jig rten sems ni bsruṅ bya ste tshig rnams kun gyis
yid ches bya
bdag gi gsan tshig gzhan mi smra

5.2 *sNar*, gyis

5.7 *sNar, Peking* bsṅad

****

One ought to know and realize everything; knowing the proper time to fear in all matters, one should protect worldly thoughts and everyone should believe in words; one should not reveal one's own secret words to others.

****

No similar verses were found in Sanskrit.

5.1 blon po blo ni phun sum tshogs
bstan bcos kun la 'jigs med cin
baṅ mdzod stobs daṅ ldan pa ni
ma bsad de yi phyir kgsaṅ 'gyur

1.2 *sNar, Peking* po'i

3.1 *sDe, Cone* dbaṅ

4.3 *sDe, Cone* der

4.4 *sDe, Cone* ni

4.6 *sDe, Cone* gsod

****

A minister who is endowed with intelligence, who is without fear towards all the *śāstras*, and who possesses resources and strength hides himself lest he be killed.

****

No similar verses were found in Sanskrit.

5.2 yid ches skyes bu 'chi 'gyur te
smig ma'i 'bras by byuṅ ba bzhin
yid ches zhags pas gsod 'gyur te
nags na gnas pa'i ri dgas bzhin

****

Trust can bring about the death of a man just as the coming forth of fruit from a bamboo (kills the bamboo); trust can bring about death with a noose just as the forest-dwelling deer was killed.

****

No similar verses were found in Sanskrit.

5.3 mig rtsa dmar zhiṅ tshig 'jam smra
dga'a bas sems can kun daṅ mthun
don rnams kun la gya gyur smra
gzhan tshig dag la 'jig rten smod

1.2 *Cone* rtsad

1.3 *Cone* mar

4.3 *sNar, Peking* gab

****

If one speaks gentle words even when one is angry, he is harmonious with everyone because of delight; but if one speaks craftily in all matters, the world blames him on the words of others.

****

No similar verses were found in Sanskrit.

5.4 de ni g-yon can spyod lam ste
de sñiṅ ñes pa chen po yis
sdig pa ni tshe'i tshogs bsags nas
groṅ gi tshogs de bzlog bya ste
groṅ khyer 'khrug byed g-yon can 'di
'byuṅ khuṅs skye bo ṅan pa'i gter
de ni 'jig rten spyi dgra yin

3.6 *sNar, Peking* bsogs

4.1 *sDe, Cone* gloṅ

4.4 *sNar, Peking* ni

4.6 *sNar, Peking* byas

4.7 *sNar, Peking* nas

****

This is indeed the path of a demon with great evil deeds; having accumulated nothing but sin he will upset the multitudes of the cities; and such a demon who disturbs the cities is the storehouse of evil people; he is the enemy of the whole world.

****

No similar verses were found in Sanskrit.

5.5 ma ruṅs skye bo kha sñan ciṅ
tsan daṅ lta bu bsil ba'i nag
sñiṅ ni ma ruṅs bdag ñid de
sog le bas kyaṅ khyad par 'phags

3.4 *sNar, Peking* ruṅ

3.6 *sNar, Peking* daṅ

4.1 *sNar, Peking* sogs

****

A rogue is characterized by sweet speech, an utterance that is as cool as sandalwood, and as for his heart it is more sharp than a saw.

****

(1) Cr 776; CS 3.27

(2) SRBh 83.59; SRK 33.81; IS 4882

****

Cr mukhaṃ padmadalākāraṃ vākyaṃ candalaśītalam
hṛdayaṃ vāhnisamyuktaṃ trividhaṃ dhurtalakṣaṇam

(b) CS, SRBh, SRK vācā; SRBh, SRK candanaśitalā

(c) CS, IS kartrīsaṃyuktaṃ; SRK, SRBh krodhasaṃyuktaṃ

5.6 ma ruṅs bdag ñid tshig 'jam zhiṅ
skyon daṅ rjes mthun sñan smra ste
mi mṅon khon bzuṅ byams med la
yid brtan byed pa gshin rdze gshed

3.6 *sDe, Cone* byed

4.2 *sNar* brten

4.4 *sNar, Peking* daṅ

4.7 *sDe, Cone* bzhin

****

The root nature of a rogue is to speak gentle words and one who trusts in the following faults is destroyed by Yama: agreeing, speaking sweetly, hiding, being angry, and being merciless.

****

The first part of this verse is similar to the Sanskrit original of verse number 3.6 in Masūrākṣa's collection. No other similar verses were found in Sanskrit.

5.7 thag riṅ mthoṅ nas mgo smod ciṅ
shin tu dam pa'i tshig brjod la
skad gsaṅ chuṅ bas smra ba ni
g-yon can rnams kyi mtshan ñid yin

1.2 *sNar, Peking* riṅs

1.4 *sNar, Peking* na

1.6 *sDe, Cone* smad

2.3 *sNar, Peking* dman

3.3 *Peking* chu

3.4 *sNar, Peking* ba

4.4 *sDe* kya

****

As for one who seeing you in the distance and bowing his head, who speaks words which are very holy, and who speaks in a low (humble) tone, he is characterized as a demon.

****

No similar verses were found in Sanskrit.

5.8 gan zhig snon chad gnod byas daṅ
de ltar gaṅ gis gnod byed pa
de la yid ches mi rigs te
khun na gnas pa'i lag 'gro bzhin

1.2 *sNar, Peking* gis

1.3 *sDe, Cone* sdon

2.1 *sNar, Peking* da

2.2 *sNar, Peking* lta

****

One should not trust someone who has done harm in the past and who makes evil in the present; such people are like snakes who live in pits.

****

No similar verses were found in Sanskrit.

5.9 'bab chu sder mo can rnams daṅ
rwa can lag na mtshon thogs daṅ
rgyal po'i pho braṅ bud med la
yid brtan bgrog par mi bya'o

1.3 *Peking* ster

****

Trust should not be put in a river, an animal with claws, an animal with horns, someone with a sword in his hand, the family of the king, or women.

****

(1) Cr 527; CV 1.15; Cv 1.16; CN 25; CS 3.48; CR 2.21; GP 1.109.14; PP .52; HJ 1.18; HM 1.18; HH 9.6-7; HS 1.17; HK 1.19

(2) SRBh 249.81; IS 3214

****

Cr nakhināṃ ca nadīnāṃ ca śṛṅgiṇāṃ śastrapāṇinām
viśvāso nāiva kartavyaḥ strīṣu rājakuleṣu ca

(a) Cv, CS, GP nadīnāṃ ca nakhīnāṃ ca; CR, SRBh nadīnāṃ nakhīnāṃ cāiva; HJ, HK, HM, HS nadīnāṃ śastrapāṇinām

(b) CR śastriṇāṃ dviṣām; HK, HK, HM, HS ṅakhīnāṃ sṛṅgināṃ tathā; PP śastradhāriṇām
(c) PP upagantavyaḥ; GP gantavyaḥ
(d) CR rājakuleṣvapi

5.10 me chu bud med blun po daṅ
sbrul daṅ rgyal rigs dag la ni
rtag tu 'bad pas sten byed pa
'phral du srog 'phrog de drug yin

1.5 *sNar, Peking* glen

1.6 *sNar, Peking* ma

****

The six things that are fatal which are to be treated with care at all times are fire, water, women, fools, snakes, and the family of the king.

****

(1) Cr 6; CV 14.12; Cv 5.19; CS 3.94; CR "S"; GP 1.114.13

(2) IS 64; MSS 200

****

Cr agnir āpaḥ striyo mūrkhāḥ sarpā rājakulāni ca
nityaṃ yatnena sevyāni sadyaḥ prāṇaharāṇi ṣaṭ

(b) CR rājakulaṃ tathā

(c) CR saṃyogasevanābhyāṃ ca; GP paropasevyāni

(d) CR, CV prāṇaharāṃ

5.11 nor rnams maṅ po ster byed pa'i
dgra la gaṅ zhig dpa'a bsten daṅ
chuṅ ma khyo la ma chags gñis
de yi 'tsho ba rab tu gcod

2.5 *sDe, Cone* brtan

2.6 *sNar, Peking* pa

4.5 *sNar, Peking* bar

4.6 *sNar, Peking* du

****

Whoever depends upon an enemy who gives out a great deal of wealth and whoever depends on a wife who does not love her husband cuts off his life.

****

No similar verses were found in Sanskrit.

5.12 sṅan chad dgrar gyur sten byed ciṅ
khon pa'i gzhi med 'khrug byed pa
grogs po'i 'dod pa bzlog byed pa'i
de dra'i grogs po riṅ du spaṅ

1.4 *sDe, Cone* 'gyur

1.5 *sNar, Peking* bshes

2.2 *sDe, Cone* pa

3.2 *sDe, Cone* po

3.5 *sDe, Cone* zlog

3.7 *sNar, Peking* pa

****

One should abandon to a distance friends who revive past enmity, who stir up unfounded hostility, and who act contrary to the desires of their friends.

****

No similar verses were found in Sanskrit.

5.13 dgra daṅ bshes gñen gyog 'khor daṅ
bar gnas rgan po ñam chuṅ rnams
rmaṅs pas bye brag mi shes pas
de ni skyes bu tha shal yin

2.5 *sNar, Peking* ñams

4.6 *sNar, Peking* shes

****

He is a vile person who does not know how to discriminate between friend and foe, those in the middle and servants, the village chief and weak ones.

****

(1) Cr 83; CS 2.18

(2) IS 7453; MSS 2855

****

Cr arim mitram udāsīnaṃ madhyasthaṃ sthaviraṃ gurum
yo na budhyati mandātmā sa ca sarvatra naśyati

****

The translators misread *dāsinaṃ* for *udāsīnaṃ* in pāda (1). They miss the comparison between the neutral person and the mediator.

5.14 rkun ma'i chos pa gsad pa daṅ
grogs 'khu myur du brjod par bya
chuṅ ma 'khu ba mal stan byed
bram ze ñes byed spyan mi draṅ

1.3 *sNar, Peking* chad

1.5 *Cone* gsod

3.7 *sNar, Peking* dbye

4.3 *sDe, Cone* shes

4.4 *sNar, Peking* med

****

One should not give an invitation to a thief, to one who has killed a holy person, to one who hates his friends, to one who can't keep secrets, to one who hates the wife who makes his bed, or to one who had harmed brahmins.

****

No similar verses were found in Sanskrit.

5.15 bdag gis mṅon sum ma gyur par
gaṅ gis ñes pa smra byed pa
gaṅ gis dmyal bar ltuṅ pa'i rgyu
las de brtsam par mi bya'o

2.1 *sNar, Peking* gzhan

4.1 *sDe, Cone* lam

4.3 *sNar, Peking* brtsams

****

One should not start an action without knowing its nature which is said to be evil or which is the cause of a falling to hell.

****

No similar verses were found in Sanskrit.

5.16 bdag ñid bdag gi gñen yin zhiṅ
bdag ñid bdag dgra yān yin
mtho ris dmyal ba de bzhin du
thams cad bdag gi dbaṅ du gnas

4.7 *sDe, Cone* bya

****

Oneself is the friend of oneself and oneself is the enemy of oneself; in the same way heaven and hell and everything else remain under the control of oneself.

****

(1) Lines 1 and 2 of this verse are the same as pādas c and d of MBh 5.34.62.
(2) Lines 1 and 2 of this verse are the same as pādas c and d of IS 893.

****

MBh ātmanātmanam anvicchen manobuddhīndriyāir yatāiḥ
ātmanāiva hy ātmano bandhur ātmanāiva ripur ātmanaḥ

(c) IS ātmā hyevātmano

6.1 blon pos legs par mñam bzhag ste
spyod pa gzhan la smra mi byed
ñi ma bzhin du dgra rnams la
gzi brjid kyis ni gduṅ bar byed

1.1 *sNar, Peking* blen

3.5 *sNar, Peking* don

****

A good minister assesses equally in all cases and will not speak about the proceedings to others, just as the sun with its brilliance gives brightness even to enemies.

****

No similar verses were found in Sanskrit.

6.2 mi srun lhan cig spyod pa dag
daṅ po dga'a zhiṅ mñan pa daṅ
bar du rtsod pas dga'a med de
tha mar sha khow zhugs pa yin

2.5 *sNar, Peking* mñen

3.7 *sDe, Cone* do

****

One who deals with evil beings at first is happy and harmonious, in the middle because of a quarrel one is without happiness, and in the end one is alienated.

****

No similar verses were found in Sanskrit.

6.3 bdag ñid tshe daṅ mtshuṅs par byed
daṅ po chuṅ dur bshes byed ciṅ
bar du de bas lhag par 'gyur
tha mar rab tu dga'a bas mdza'a

1.3 *sNar, Peking* cha

1.6 *sNar, Peking* pa

1.7 *sNar, Peking* yin

2.4 *sNar, Peking* du

4.7 *sNar, Peking* mdzad

****

Friendship is like life itself, at first it is small, in the middle it is greater, and finally it consists of great pleasure.

****

No similar verses were found in Sanskrit.

6.4 dam pa'i bshes ni 'bab chu 'dra
dań po myur zhiń rab tu che
rim gyis rim gyis rgya cher' phel
'gro ba phyir ni bzlog pa med

1.5 *sNar, Peking* bar

2.3 *sNar, Peking* ñun

4.2 *sNar, Peking* ba'i

4.5 *sNar, Peking* ldog

4.6 *sNar, Peking* tu

****

The friendship of a good person is like a river; at first it is swift and great; in the middle step by step it increases in size and it goes forward without returning.

****

No similar verses were found in Sanskrit.

6.5 dud 'gro dri yis mthoń bar byed
rig byed kyis ni bram ze mthoń
sman gyi rig pas sman pa mthoń
rgyal po ñan rnams mthoń bar byed

3.3 *sNar, Peking* rigs

****

An animal sees by means of his sense of smell; a brahmin sees by means of the Vedas; a doctor sees by means of his medical techniques; a king sees by means of spies.

****

(1) Cr 1422; MBh 5.34.32; PP 3.58; PKB 3.67

(2) IS 2084; SS ARthaparva 137.9

****

Cr gandhena gāvaḥ paśyanti vedāih paśyanti brāhmaṇāh
cārāiḥ paśyanti rājānaś cakṣurbhyām itare janāḥ

(b) PKB, IS vāi dvijāḥ: SS bhūsurāḥ

(c) PP carāiḥ

****

The Sanskrit reads: Cows see with their sense of smell; brahmins see by means of the vedas; kings see by means of spies; likewise people (see) with their two eyes.

6.6 mi yis dgra ni gzhom 'dod pas
rtag tu sñan smra dran pa bsam
glu yis briṅ pa'i ri dags bzhin
sems 'khrul 'gyur nas gsad par bya

1.2 *sDe, Cone* yi

3.1 *sNar, Peking* klu

4.5 *sNar, Peking* bsad

****

One should always speak good things to that enemy whom one desires to conquer, just as a deer having been charmed by the song is killed.

****

(1) Cr 825; CV 14.10

(2) SRBh 247.7; SV 2759; SP 1428; IS 5367

****

SV yasya cāpriyam anvicched brūyāt tasya sadā priyam
vyādhā mṛgavadhaṃ kartuṃ hṛdyaṃ gāyanti susvaram

(a) Cr, CV yasmāc ca priyam iccheta

(b) SRBh, SP tasya kuryāt; Cr, CV, IS tasya brūyāt

(c) CV vyādho

(d) CV gītaṃ gāyati; SRBh, IS samyag; Cr, SP gītaṃ gāyanti

6.7 gaṅ la nor yod bshes gñen daṅ
gaṅ la nor yod ñe du ste
gaṅ la nor yod 'jog rten mi
gaṅ la nor yod de mdzaṅs yin

1.5 *sNar, Peking* gñen

1.6 *sNar, Peking* bshes

****

There are friends for the one who has wealth; there are relatives for the one who has wealth; the person who has wealth is a man in the world; a wise man is one who has wealth.

****

(1) Cr 844; Cv 6.8; CV 7.15; CR 4.12; MBh 12.8.19; GP 1.111.17; PRE 2.31; PS 2.31; PTK 2.52; PKB 1.3; HJ 1.133; HP 1.95; HM 1.124; HH 25.24-5; HS 1.118; HK 1.127

(2) SV 2816; SRBh 95.6; SRK 52.7; IS 5409; SS Arthaparva 100.1

****

Cr yasyārthās tasya mitrāṇi yasyārthās tasya bāndhavāḥ
yasyārthaḥ sa pumāṃ loke yasyārthāḥ sa ca paṇḍitaḥ

(d) CV, Cv jivati; CR, HK, HM sa hi; HJ, HH sa tu

6.8 nor med gyur na gñen bshes daṅ
bu daṅ chuṅ ma ñe du daṅ
skye bo sdug pa rnams kyis spoṅ
nor ldan gyur na phyir yaṅ gñen
nor ni 'jig rten mi yi gñen

1.5 *sDe, Cone* gnan

4.7 *sDe, Cone* bsten

****

Friends, sons, wife, relatives, and good men abandon one who has lost his wealth; when he obtains wealth again he obtains (friends, etc.) again; indeed wealth is man's friend in the world.

****

(1) Cr 429; CV 15.5; Cv 6.9; GP 1.111.18; PP 2.106; PRE 2.33; PT 2.54

(2) SRBh 93.11; SRK 52.15; is 2622

****

Cr tyajanti mitrāṇi dhanāir vihīnaṃ
putrāś ca dārāś ca suhṛjjanāś ca
tam arthavantaṃ punar āśrayante
artho hi loke puruṣasya bandhuḥ

(a) PP PRE dhanena hīnaṃ

(b) PP, PRE sahodarās; IS dārāśca bhṛtās; Cv dārāśca putrāś

(c) PP, PRE eva yanti; CV, IS te ca; Cv, GP āśrayanti

(d) CR apyartho hi; SRK, SRBh hyartho; PP, PRE hyartho 'tra

6.9 go 'phaṅ mchog thob gyur na ni
bshes gñen grogs po la sogs pa
sṅon ma mthoṅ ba rnams kyaṅ 'dud
nor zad go 'phaṅ ñams due na
raṅ mi rnams kyaṅ dgrar 'gyur ro

2.7 *sNar, Peking* pa'i

3.7 *sNar, Peking* bdud

5.7 *sDe, Cone* la

sDE and *Cone* also contain two additional lines:

nor daṅ mi ldan skye bo yis
bden pa smras kyaṅ bar byed

****

When one obtains the highest rank, friends, relations, acquaintances, etc. who were previously not present pay reverence; at the time of the destruction of this high position and loss of wealth, even one's own men will become hostile.

****

(1) Cr 37; CR 2.13; GP 1.109.7

(2) MSS 845

****

Cr adṛṣṭapūrvā bahavaḥ sahāyāḥ
sarve padasthasya bhavanti vaśyāḥ
arthād vihīnasya padacyutasya
bhavanti kāle svajano 'pi śatruḥ

(b) GP mitrāḥ

(c) GP arthāir

(d) GP bhavatyakāle

6.10 gsaṅ ṅam khoṅ ni grims pa daṅ
brnag pa mthar phyin byed nus daṅ
dgra la rigs pa spyod pa ni
dgra bo 'jigs 'gyur the tshom med

2.6 *sDe, Cone* dus

3.3 *sNar, Peking* 'jigs

****

A person who conceals his secrets inside and is capable of total hatred and who acts properly towards his enemies unquestionably makes the enemies afraid.

****

No similar verses were found in Sanskrit.

6.11 dgra yi phyogs la mkhas pa yis
dań bor rtsa ba gcad par bya
de nas rań gi phyogs bcas pas
sdon chad gnod pa byed pa gsad

2.2 *sDe, Cone* bo

****

He who knows about the ways of his enemy first investigates the cause of the enmity and then according to his strength he destroys those who did him harm in former times.

****

(1) Cr 1011; CR 5.26; GP 1.112.22

****

Cr saṇmāsam athavā varṣsaṃ saṃdhiṃ kuryān narādhipaḥ
ātmano balam ālokya paścāc chatruṃ nipātayet

(a) GP varṣaṃ vā

(c) GP paśyan sañcitamātmanaṃ

(d) GP punaḥ

****

The Sanskrit verse has a slightly different idea in pādas a and b.

6.12 gań zhig dgrar 'gyur skye bo dań
slar ni 'dum par 'dod gyur pa
de ni 'chi ba ñer len te
dre'u mo yi ni mńal bzhin no

1.1 *sNar, Peking* lan

1.2 *sNar, Peking* cig

1.3 *sNar, Peking* 'jigs

1.5 *sNar, Peking* bshes

1.6 *sNar, Peking* gñen

1.7 *sNar, Peking* gań

****

That person who would desire friendship again with a man who was previously hostile obtains death, just as the pregnancy of a mule (will kill it).

****

(1) Cr 1024; CN 17; CR 3.15; GP 1.110.19; PP 2.27, 4.13; PRE 2.19; Ps 2.19; PT 2.29; PKB 2.32; 4.14; HJ 2.146; HP 2.135; HM 2.148; HH 65.11-2; HS 2.140; HK 2.146
(2) SRBh 260.362; SV 2757; IS 6656; SS Arthaparva 76.3

****

Cr sakṛdduṣṭaṃ ca mitraṃ yaḥ punaḥ saṃdhātum icchati
sa mṛtyum upagṛhṇāti garbham aśvatraī yathā

(a) CR, PRE, PS, PT, PTK, HM, HS, HK tu yo mitraṃ; GP, PP 2.27, PKB 4.14 ca yo mitraṃ; HP, HH tu yan mitraṃ; PKB 2.32 apiṣṭaṃ; HJ yo tu mitraṃ; SV duṣṭas tu yaḥ kaścit; SS dviṣṭaṃ to yo 'mitram
(c) GP eva gṛhṇīyād; PP 2.27, HP, HJ, HH, HS, HK eva gṛhṇāti
(d) PP 2.27 garbhād

6.13 dgra daṅ lhan cig 'dum byed ciṅ
yid brtan bde bar gñid log pa
de ni shiṅ rtser gñid log pa
lhuṅ nas gsad pa ji bzhin no

1.3 *sNar, Peking* lan

3.7 *sNar, Peking* pa'i

4.3 *sNar, Peking* sad

****

A person who makes peace with an enemy and who then falls asleep trustingly is like one who falls asleep at the top of a tree and having fallen off is killed.

****

(1) Cr 964; CR 7,.44; CS 1.8; MBh 12.138.37; GP 1.114.48; HJ 4.11; HP 4.11; HM 4.10; HH 101.17-8; HS 4.8; HK 4.11

(2) SV 2756; IS 6293; SS Arthaparva 61.10

****

Mbh yo 'riṇāsaha saṃdhāya sukhaṃ svapiti viśvasān
sa vṛkṣāgraprasupto vāpatitaḥ pratibudhyate

(a) Cr, CR, CS, GP vāriniā; CS viśvāsam; HP praṇāmādupahārādvā; HM, HH, HS, HK, HJ praṇayādupakārādvā
(b) Cr, CS yo naraḥ kartumicchati; CR viśvasto yaḥ svapet sukham; GP viśvati yadi tiṣṭhati; HP, HM, HS, HJ, HK yo viśvasiti śatruṣu; HH yo viśvasati śatruṣu; SS viśvasta sthātum icchati
(c) Cr, CS vṛkṣāgreṣu saṃsuptaḥ; CR vṛkṣagreṣu kṛtasvapnaḥ; GP vṛkṣāgre prasupto hi; HP supta iva vṛkṣāgre; HJ, HM, HK supta iva vṛkṣGauhatirāt; HH prasupta iva vṛkṣāgrāt; HS prasupta iva vṛkṣāgre; SV vṛkṣāgre; supta iva; SS sa supta iva vṛkṣāgrāt

6.14 gal te bu 'm spun zla 'm
snag gi gñen mtshams 'grogs bshes rnams
rgyal po'i bar dụ gcod byed na
gsad byar 'di the tshom med

3.2 *sDe, Cone* por

4.2 *sNar, Peking* bya

****

If a son, brother, relative, in-law, or close friend should come in the way of a king, there is no doubt that that one will be killed.

****

(1) PP 1.428; PRE 1.173; PS 1.153; PTK 1.182; PT 1.169; PKB 1.423; HJ 2.177; HP 2.161; HM 2.178; HH 7016-7; HS 2.169; HK 2.176
(2) SRBh 237.227; IS 4069

****

PP pitā vā yadī vā bhrātā putro vā yadi vā suhṛt
prāṇadrohe pravṛttaḥ san hantavyo bhūtim icchatā

(b) PT, PTK bhāryā putro 'thavā; PKB bhāryāthavā
(c) PRE prāṇadrohakārā tājñā; PS prāṇadrohakaro rājñam; PT, PTK vartamānā; PKB prāṇadroham yadā gacchet; HJ, HP, HM, HH, HS, HK prāṇacchedakarā rājñā
(d) PRE, PT, PTK, HJ, HP, HM, HH, HS, HK hantavyā; PS chettavyo; PKB tam ghnato nāsti pātakam

6.15 mñen pas mi mñen 'jig pa ste
'jam pos rtsub pa 'jig par byed
mñen bas mi 'dul cuṅ zad med
de bas mñen pa shin tu rno

1.4 *sNar, Peking* gnan

3.1 *sNar, Peking* gñen

4.3 *sNar, Peking* gñen

4.7 *sNar, Peking* no

****

A gentle thing is destroyed by gentle means; a rough thing is destroyed by gentle means; there is nothing that can't be destroyed by gentle means; nothing is sharper than gentle means.

****

(1) Cr 788; CS 3.40; MBh 12.138.65; GP 1.114.49 (cd, ab)

(2) IS 4964

****

CS mṛdunāiva mṛdum hanti mṛdunā hanti dāruṇam
nāsathyaṃ mṛdunā kimcit tasmāt tīkṣnataraṃ mṛduḥ

(a) Cr, GP mṛduneva mṛduṃ; MBh mṛdunā sumṛduṃ; IS chinddha

(d) Cr, GP, MBh mṛdu; IS tīkṣṇataro

6.16 nor mñam nus pa mñam pa daṅ
gnas la mkhas shiṅ brtson 'grus che
rgyal srid dṅos su 'phrog pa'i mi
gal te ma bsad des gsod 'gyur

1.5 *sNar, Peking* ñams
3.3 *sNar, Peking* phyed
3.4 *sNar, Peking* ni

****

If a king does not kill one among his officers who is equal in wealth, who is equal in strength, who is learned in different fields, who is very industrious, and who openly seizes the kingdom, then he will be killed.

****

(1) Cr 420; GP 1.112.17; CR 5.21; PKB 1.248

(2) SRBh 234.159; IS 2584; SP 1367

****

CR tulyārthaṃ tulyasāmarthyaṃ mantrajñaṃ vyavasāyinam
ardharājyaharaṃ bhṛtyaṃ yo na hanyātsa hanyate

(b) Cr, PKB, GP, SP, IS marmajñaṃ; SRBh sarvajñaṃ

6.17 zab mo blo ldan ṅag 'jam zhiṅ
dman par smra la dbaṅ po thul
bden par smra zhiṅ gzhan dbaṅ can
shis pa'i tshig ldan de ñid rig
de 'dra'i gyog 'khor bzaṅ po yin

1.2 *sNar, Peking* mo'i

1.3 *sNar, Peking* glo

1.5 *sNar, Peking* daṅ

5.2 *sNar, Peking* ñid

The *sDe dGe* and the *Cone* additions insert the following line between lines 4 and 5:

rje bo la ni rtag gus pas

****

Those servants are useful who possess a deep intellect, whose speech is gentle, who speak in a low voice, who restrain their *indriyas*, who speak the truth, who remain under the power of others, who speak auspicious words and who know the real state of things.

****

(1) Cr 339; CR 5.22; GP 1.112.18

****

Cr gāmbhīryayuktā mṛdumandavākyā
jitendriyāḥ satyaparāḥ suyogāḥ
bhāvyarthatajjñā viditārthatattvāḥ
prāyeṇa bhṛtyāḥ kṛtināṃ bhavanti

(a) GP śūratvyuktā

(b) GP satyaparākramāśca

(c) GP prāgeva paścādviparītarūpā

(d) GP ye te bhṛtyā na hitā

6.18 shin tu chog shes le lo med
legs par gñid lod rab tu sad
bde daṅ sdug bsṅal grogs byed pa'i
gyog 'khor 'jig rten rab tu dkon

1.3 *sDe, Cone* mchog

****

It is very difficult to find servants in the world who are easily satisfied, who aren't lazy, who go to sleep easily, who wake easily, and who accept happiness as well as suffering.

****

(1) Cr 609; CR 5.23; GP 1.112.19

****

Cr nirālasyāḥ susaṃtuṣṭāḥ susvapnāḥ suprabodhinaḥ
sukhaduḥkhasamā dhīrā bhṛtyā jagati durlabhāḥ

(b) GP pratibodhikāḥ

(d) GP lokeṣu

6.19 g-yo can rnams la g-yo ston ciṅ
draṅ la draṅ ba'i spyod pa ston
dga'a daṅ dga'a ba ñid daṅ ni
mi dga'a ba la mi dga'a ston

1.3 *sNar, Peking* dag

3.4 *sNar, Peking* ba'i

****

Be cunning towards those who possess cunning; behave honestly towards those who are honest; be happy with happy people; behave in an unhappy manner towards those who are unhappy.

****

No similar verses were found in Sanskrit.

6.20 dṅos po gaṅ la gaṅ dga'a ba'i
skyes pa bud med ston byed pa
dam pa rnams kyi 'jug sgo ni
nam du yaṅ ni mi 'dor to

2.2 *sDe, Cone* pa'm

2.7 *sNar, Peking* pa'o

****

One should never reject the direction of holy men who are the guides for men and women who take delight in whatever material things (they have).

****

No similar verses were found in Sanskrit.

6.21 skye bo ṅan dan 'gros na ni
skye bo dam pa'an ñams byed de
chu daṅ 'dam bu 'dres na ni
daṅ ba'aṅ dri ma can du 'gyur

3.4 *sDe, Cone* du

****

When there is friendship with an evil person even a good person becomes harmed, just as water even though it is clean that is mixed with swamp reeds becomes tainted.

****

(1) Cr 474; CR 3.30

(2) IS 7546

****

Cr durjanāiḥ saha saṅgena sajjano 'pi vinaśyati
jalaṃ prasannam apyāhuḥ paṅkaḥ kaluṣatāṃ nayet

(c) IS prasannaṃ jalamity

(d) IS kardamāiḥ kaluṣāyate

6.22 kha la sbraṅ rtsis bsgos bzhin daṅ
knon na rñog pa'i bdag ñid de
naṅna ra gaṅ phyir dṅul daṅ
kha yi naṅ gi rdo phye bzhin

3.3 *sNar, Peking* rag

3.4 *sDe, Cone* phyi

3.5 *sNar, Peking* rdul

3.7 *sDe, Cone* lam

****

One who is (sweet) like honey in speech, but whose self is internally troubled is like one who has brass on the inside and silver on the outside and ground stone inside his mouth.

****

No similar verses were found in Sanskrit.

6.23 tshig 'jam brtse med shes rab ldan
mi mṅom shin tu mi bzad pa
bu ram dụg 'dres lta bu yi
de dra'i skyes bu bsten mi bya

2.5 *Peking* ma

4.5 *sNar, sDe, Peking* bstan

****

One should not serve a person who speaks soft words but has not love and who possesses wisdom but is secretive and very irritable, such a person is like a mixture of molasses and poison.

****

No similar verses were found in Sanskrit.

6.24 shin tu ma ruṅs skye bo la
rjes su mthun pas zhi bya zhiṅ
sṅar ba'i dag gis bsgo bya ste
mkhris pa'i naṅ 'byuṅ ji bzhin no

3.1 *sDe, Cone* mṅar

3.5 *sNar*, bsgos; *Peking* bgos

3.6 *sNar, Peking* byas

3.7 *sNar, Peking* te

****

If you were to make peace by means of an agreement with a rogue, it would be as if you defiled what was previously clean by soaking it in a bilious fluid.

****

No similar verses were found in Sanskrit. This verse is somewhat similar to verse 6.21.

6.25 nya gro dha zhes bya ba yi
syiṅ gi rgyal por grags pa yod
de yi myu gu bu rnams ni
rtsa ba zugs nas gtiṅ gnas te
gcig la gcig ni 'brel byas nas
de nas shiṅ de 'gij par 'gyur
de bzhin bu daṅ tsha bo daṅ
blon bo'i tshogs daṅ bcas pa yi
rgyal po gnas nas skyod byed de
nya gro dha yi myu gu bzhin

1.7 *Peking* yis

8.7 *sNar, Peking* yis

9.2 *sNar, Peking* po'i

****

That which is known as the Nyagrodha tree (banyan tree) is famous as the king of trees; its small sprouts can pierce its roots, can become established below the tree, can become tangled together, and eventually can destroy the tree. Likewise the king who has a host of sons, grandsons, and ministers is driven out of his residence in the manner of the sprouts of the Nyagrodha tree.

****

No similar verses were found in Sanskrit.

7.1 sa bdag gi ni g-yog 'khor gyi
mtshan ñid bshad kyis mñan par gyis
rgyal po ji ltar shes ñen ldan
g-yog 'khor de ltar brtag par bya

3.6 *sNar, Peking* gñen

****

This chapter enumerates the essential marks of servants of kings; thus that king who is warned will thereby examine his servants.

****

(1) cr 660; CR 4.1; Cv 4.7; CS 1.64; GP 1.111.1

****

CR pārthivasya ca bhṛtyasya vadāmi guṇalakṣaṇam
yena saṃvardhate rājā bhāṇḍāgāras tathāiva ca

(a) Cr, CR pārthivasya pravakṣyāmi; Cv, GP tu vakṣyāmi

(b) Cr, GP, CR bhṛtyānāṃ cāiva lakṣaṇam; Cv bhṛtyānāṃ

(c) GP sarvāṇi hi; Cr, CR yathābhijño mahīpālah; Cv rājyaṃ

(d) GP nityaṃ parīkṣayet; Cr, CR samyag bhṛtyān prapālayet

7.2 ji ltar dbaṅ po la sogs pa'i
mi ni lha rnams kun gyi kha
de bzhin rgyal po'i blon po yaṅ
yul 'khor rgyu daṅ mi rgyu'i kha

****

Just as Indra and his retinue are the foremost of men and gods, just so a royal minister is at the head of all things moving and unmoving.

****

No similar verses were found in Sanskrit.

7.3 brtan zhiṅ zab mo'i blo daṅ ladn
mdaṅs ldan chos daṅ bstan bcos rig
dul zhiṅ bden par smra ba daṅ
rgyal po'i 'khor la phan par sems
rigs btsun rgyud ni mñen pa daṅ
bla ma la ni gus ñan daṅ
skye dgu rjes brtser ldan pa yi
rgyud byuṅ de ni rgyal sras yin

1.2 *Peking* ciṅ

2.6 *sNar* chos

7.2 *sNar, Peking* dgu'i

8.6 *sDe, Cone* sems

****

The eight characteristics of a king's son are the possession of an intellect that is firm and deep, knowledge of *dharma* and the *śāstras*, possession of self-control, truthful speech, the knowledge of useful characteristics of servants, respectable family heritage, ability to listen respectfully to holy men, and compassion for all beings.

****

No similar verses were found in Sanskrit.

7.4 rgyal po sñiṅ rje phan sems ldan
bla ma'i skyon ni sbed pa daṅ
gyul 'jug slar yaṅ mi ldog ciṅ
bde daṅsdug bsṅal mñam par shes

1.4 *sNar, Peking* brtse

****

A king should possess thoughts of compassion and welfare, should keep secret the faults of holy men, should not go to battle unnecessarily, and should possess a mind that is the same in joy and in misery.

****

No similar verses were found in Sanskrit.

7.5 rigs daṅ tshul khrims phun sum tshogs
chos lugs 'chad pa mjhas pa ste
de bzhin dul daṅdad pa daṅ
grims pa rgyal por rab grags so

3.3 *sNar, Peking* 'dun

****

A king becomes famous who is from a good family, who possesses morals, grace, glory, and wealth, who follows the *dharma*, who is skilled in explaining *nīti*, and who is likewise disciplined, devoted, and skillful.

****

(1) JH 1.213; HP 1.159; HM 1.198; HH 36. 1-2; HS 1.193; HK 1.200
(2) SRBh 233.118; IS 5005; SRK 143.3

****

HJ yaḥ kulābhijanācārāir atiśuddaḥ pratāpavān
dhārmiko nītikuśalaḥ sa svāmī yujyate bhuyi

(a) HP kulīno janācārāir; HH, HJ kulācārajanācārāir

7.6 tshig gsal blo ni phun sum tshogs
lugs kyi bstan bcos dag la mkhas
daṅ 'jam spyod par byed pa ste
rgyal po'i blon po de 'dres bya

2.4 *Cone* 'cos

3.3 *sDe, Cone* dpyod

****

A royal minister should act as follows: he should have clear speech, perfect intellect, skill in the *nītiśāstras*, and the practice of gentle speech.

****

No similar verses were found in Sanskrit.

7.7 yid gzhuṅs tshig gsal shes rab ldan
gzhan sems ñe bar mtshon nus daṅ
brtan zhiṅ ji skad bsgo bzhin smra
rgyal po'i pho ña de 'dras byas

****

A royal messenger should be one who has an attentive mind, clear speech, and wisdom, who is capable of scrutinizing the thoughts of others, who is firm, and who speaks as he is ordered.

****

(1) Cr 789; CN 104; CS 1.63; Cv 44.9

(2) SRBh 231.70; IS 4979

****

Cr medhāvī vākpaṭuḥ prājñaḥ pracittopalakṣakaḥ
dhīro yathoktavādī ca eṣa dūto vidhīyate

(a) Cv prvīṇaḥ prekṣaṇe dakṣaḥ

(c) Cv sphuṭvākyaḥ tathā prājña

7.8 rig byed yan lag de ñid shes
bzlas brjod spyin sreg mchod tu brtson
rtag tu shis pa rjod byed pa
shes rab ldan de mdun na 'don

2.5 *sDe, Cone* mchog

3.3 *sNar, Peking* shiṅ

****

A *purohita* priest should know the essence of the *veda* and its limbs, should make efforts to recite *mantras*, make offerings, make oblations, and should always speak words of blessing.

****

(1) Cr 963; Cv 4.8; CN 99; CS 1.52; CR 5.13; GP 1.112.12

(2) SRBh 228.18; IS 6269; SP 1333; SS ARthaparva 45.4

****

CR vedavedāṅgatattvajño japahomaparāyaṇaḥ
āśīrvādaparo nityameṣa rājñaḥ purohitaḥ

(c) SS āśīrvādarato

(d) CN, GP, SS, SRBh rājapurohitaḥ; CR pārthivasya

7.9 sgra rig rtsis kyaṅ shes pa ste
yi ge byaṅ zhiṅ lag pa myur
yid gzhuṅs tshig ni gsal ba daṅ
grags daṅ spyin ldan yi ge pa

2.3 *Peking* bya

4.7 *Peking* ba

****

A scribe who knows grammar and counting, is clever with letters, has a fast hand, has an attentive mind, and has clear speech will become famous and receive gifts.

****

(1) Cr 1023; CN 102; CS 1.59

(2) SRBh 231.76; IS 6654

****

Cr sakṛduktagṛhītārtho laghuhasto jitākṣaraḥ
sarvaśāstrasamālokī prakṛṣṭo nāma lekhakaḥ

(c) SRBh śabdaśāstra parijñātā

(d) SRBh eṣa lekhaka iṣyate

7.10 yi ge bzaṅ zhiṅ sgra la mkhas
sgra yi mtshan ñid rtogs byed ciṅ
dri za bzhin du dbyaṅs mkhas te
de 'dra'i klog mkhan bsgo bar bya

2.7 *sNar, Peking* de

****

One should seek out a singer who is skilled in using letters and words, who can discriminate the characteristics of words, and who is skilled in melodious song like the *gandharvas*.

****

No similar verses were found in Sanskrit.

7.11 brtan zhiṅ dbaṅ po rjes su 'os
shes rab che zhiṅ legs ñes rtogs
gcaṅ zhiṅ rgyal po'io sku byed sten
de 'dra chad pa gcod mkhan yin

1.4 *sDe, Cone* por

1.5 *sNar, Peking* rje

3.6 *sDe, Cone* phyed

3.7 *sDe, Cone* brten

4.2 *sNar, Peking* 'dra'i

4.6 *sDe, Cone* byed

****

A body-guard should be firm, as worthy and Indra, wise, able to discriminate between good and evil, pure, and a server of the king's body.

****

No similar verses were found in Sanskrit.

7.12 tshe yi rig byed goms pa daṅ
chos rig yid 'oṅ sñan smra zhiṅ
cho ga daṅ tshul phun sum tshogs
thaṅ la 'bar bzhin gso mkhas shiṅ
nad kyi mtshan ñid kun la mkhas
rgyal pos de 'dra'i sman pa bsten

6.2 *sDe, Cone* po

6.7 *sDe, Cone* bstan

****

A king should depend on a doctor who is skilled in Ayurvedic medicine, who is mindful of *dharma*, who is an eminent speaker, who has a perfect natural temperament and behavior, who is as skilled in curing disease as a blaze of fire, and who is skilled in all signs of disease.

****

(1) Cr 149; Cv 4.11; CN 101; CS 1.57; CR 5.11; GP 1.112.11

(2) SRBh 228.20; IS 999; MSS 5156; SS ARthaparva 48.7

****

Cr āyurvedakṛtābhyāsaḥ sarveṣāṃ priyadarśanaḥ
āryaśīlaguṇopeta eṣa vāidyo vidhīyate

(b) CR sarvatra; CS, SS sarvajñaḥ

(c) Cv uktahetusamāyukta; CR dṛṣṭzalakṣyaḥ suśīlaśca; GP āyuhśīlaguṇopeto; SS arthaśīlaguṇopeta

(d) CR prājñaśca bhiṣagucyate; GP vāidyo eṣa

7.13 gzhan gyi spyod lam zur gyis shes
stobs ldan sñan par smra pa daṅ
zhan gyi bsam pa rtag tu shes
sgo dpon de 'dra bsgo bar bya

4.1 *sNar, Peking* rgod

****

The door keeper should be instructed to know the gestures of others, should be strong, should speak praise, and should always know the thoughts of others.

****

(1) Cr 162; CN 106; CS 1.60; CR 5.5; GP 1.112.6

(2) SRBh 231.77; IS 1089; MSS 5748; SP 1337

****

CR ingitākāratattvajño balavān pryiadarśanaḥ
apramādī sadā dakṣaḥ pratīhāraḥ sa ucyate

(c) CR mahārthaśca; GP pramāthī ca; SP samayajñaḥ svāmibhaktaḥ

7.14 mtshon la goms shiṅ nus daṅ ldan
bzhon pa dgal bya bzhin mjhas
dba'a zhiṅ brtan pa phun sum tshogs
de 'dra dmag dpon yin par sges

2.6 *sNar, Peking* zhiṅ

2.7 *sDe, Cone* goms

****

He is known as the army commander who possesses the ability of fighting with a sword, who is skilled in horsemanship, and who is endowed with respect and firmness.

****

(1) Cr 2044; 1045; CS 1.61, 1.62; CN 103; Cv 4.13; GP 1.112.16

(2) IS 6841; SRBh 229.33

****

CN samastaśastraśāstrajño vāhaneṣu jitaśramaḥ
sāuryavīryaguṇopetaḥ senādhyakṣo vidhīyate

(a) CS 1.61 samastakṛtaśāstrajño; CS 1.62; Cr 1045; Cv samastahayaśāstrajño; Cr 1044 samastayuddhaśāstrajño; SRBh samastanītiśāstrajño; GP samastasmṛtiśāstrajño

(b) CS 1.61, CR 1044 paṇḍitaśca; CS 1.62 parājitaḥ; SRBh vāhane pūjitasramaḥ; GP paṇḍito 'tha jitendriyaḥ

(c) Cr 1044, CS 1.61 dhāiryasāuryaguṇopetaḥ

(d) CR 1045, CS 1.62, Cv asvādhyakṣo; GP dharmādhyakṣo

7.15 pha mes rgyud byuṅ grims par shes
bstan bcos rig ciṅ zhim par 'tshed
gtsaṅ smra che zhiṅsñiṅ ñe bar
de lta bu yis phyag tshad bya

1.4 *sNar, Peking* 'byuṅ

1.7 *sNar* bshor; *Peking* bshod

2.3 *sNar* rigs

3.2 *sDe, Cone* sbra

3.7 *sNar, Peking* ba'i

****

The cook should have an hereditary position, be skillful, know the *śāstras*, know how to cook sweet things, have clear speech,and be friendly.

****

(1) Cr 665; Cv 4.10; CN 105; CS 1.58; CR 5.10; GP 1.112.10

(2) SRBh 231.78; IS 4111

****

Cr pitṛpāitāmaho dakṣaḥ śāstrajño miṣṭapācakaḥ
ssatyaśāucasamāyuktaḥ sūpakāraḥ sa ucyate

(a) CN, SRBh, IS patrapāutraguṇopetaḥ

(b) GP satyavācakaḥ

(c) CN, CS, GP, SRBh, IS śūraśca kaṭhinaśāiva; CR śāucayuktaḥ prabhorbhaktaḥ

(d) CS praśasyate; CR abhidhīyate

7.16 shes cher dpyad med phun sum tshogs
bstan bcos kun la 'jigs med daṅ
rigs ni chen por skyes gyur pa
de ni naṅ blon shes par bya

****

A prime minister should be known as one who has perfection in many distinctive knowledges, one who is not intimidated by all the *śāstras*, and whose lineage is of a noble family.

****

No similar verses were found in Sanskrit.

7.17 loṅ ba 'phye bo theṅ po daṅ
sñiṅ ñe brtan la rtag 'grus te
ri bo bzhin du mi 'gul ba
de 'dras btsun mo'i sruṅ ma bya

This verse does not appear in either the *sNar Thang* or the *Peking* edition of the *bsTan 'Gyur.*

****

The queen's guard should not be blind, crippled, or lame, should always be enthusiastic in regard to steadfast devotion, and should be as unshakable as a mountain.

****

No similar verses were found in Sanskrit.

7.18 lus kyi 'gyur ba bcas pa yis
glu tshig lam la mkhas pa daṅ
gar daṅ sdeb sbyor mchog shes pa
de 'dra'i sruṅ mkhan bsten par bya

4.3 *sNar, Peking* bsruṅ

Lines 1, 2, and 3 of this verse are not included in either the *sNar Thang* or the *Peking* editions of the *bsTan 'Gyur.*

****

The guardian should be one who is endowed with physical dexterity, who is skilled in music, and who knows dance and poetry.

****

No similar verses were found in Sanskrit.

7.19 brtan zhiṅ rgyal ba 'thob pa daṅ
gdugs dkar ba daṅ dkar ba ste
gyul las rtag par rgyal ba ni
rgyal po'i bu zhes rab tu grags

1.1 *sDe, Cone* bstan

1.5 *sNar, Peking* thob

3.7 *sNar, Peking* ste

4.3 *sNar, Peking* zhes

4.4 *sNar, Peking* sa

****

One who is steadfast, who obtains victories, who has a white umbrella, and who is always victorious in battle is known as the (true) son of a king.

****

No similar verses were found in Sanskrit.

7.20 ji ltar khyi zhig bkres ñen te
rus ba skam po khar bcaṅs nas
khrag byuṅ sdug bsṅal bde sñam pa
de bzhin 'dod rmoṅs rnams kyis ni
bud med rnams la bde sñam sems

2.6 *sNar, Peking* brdzaṅs
5.5 *sNar, Peking* bder

****

Just as a dog being sick and hungry thinks there is pleasure holding a dry bone in its mouth from the arising of its own blood, just so one who is deluded by desire thinks that there is pleasure in women.

****

(1) PP 1.12; PRE 1.9; PS 1.10; PTK 1.7; PT 1.4; HJ 2.39; HP 2.36; HM 2.41; HH 46.7-10; HS 2.39; HK 2.41
(2) SRBh 114.21; IS 7322

****

PP svalpasnāyuvasāvaśeṣamalinaṃ nirmāṃsam apy asthikaṃ
śvā labdhvā paritoṣam eti na ca tat tasya kṣudhāsāntaye

siṃho jambukam aṅkam āgatam api tyaktvā nihanti dvipaṃ
sarvaḥ kṛcchragato 'pi vañchati janaḥ sattvānurūpaṃ phalam

(a) PT, IS svalpaṃ; HH, HS, HJ alpasnāyu; PRE, PS, PT, PTK, SRBh, IS asti goḥ
(b) HK, SRBh tu; PRE, PTK, HM, HS, SRBh kṣudhaḥ seantaye; HH kṣudhā śāntaye; HP, HM, HH, HS (na) bhavet

****

Note: The Tibetan verse omits some of the *upamās* which are in the Sanskrit verse (the lion and the jackal) and changes the punch line to a statement against women.

Notes

1. *sNar Thang bsTan 'Gyur mDo*. Bundle Co 203b1-209a5(Harvard Yenching Library Collection).
2. *sDE dGe bsTan 'Gyur mDo*. Bundle Ṅo 137b6-143a7. (Harvard Yenching Library Collection).
3. Suzuki, D.T. (Editor). *The Tibetan Tripitaka-Peking Edition*. Tokyo: Suzuki Research Foundation, 1962. (Indiana University Library VQ 1250. S954 1955. Vo. 144, p. 1921).
4. *Cone Tanjur*. (Microfiche Edition). New York: The Institute for Advanced Studies of World Religions. LMpj 020, 125 5/9. Vol. 124 (Ṅo) 132a7-137a6.
5. Kenneth Ch'en, "The Tibetan Tripitaka" in *Harvard Journal of Asiatic Studies* Vol. IX (1946), p. 53-54.
6. *Ibid.*, p. 54.
7. H. Hoffmann, *Tibet, A Handbook*. (Bloomington: Indiana University Press, 1975), p. 203.
8. Ch'en, "*The Tibetan Tripitaka*," p. 58-59.
9. Hoffmann, *Tibet*, p. 203
10. Ch'en, "*The Tibetan Tripitaka*," p. 58.
11. L. Sternbach, *Cāṇakya-Nīti-Text Tradition* (Hoshiarpur: Vishneshvaranand Vedic Research Institute, 1967-1970).

5

Available evidence points to some conclusions concerning the composition and proliferation of the *Nītiśāstra* of Masūrākṣa. It appears that the Sanskrit verses were compiled around the middle of the ninth century in Bengal. The compiler was in all likelihood a son-in-law of the great Pāla king Dharmapāla. Masūrākṣa served as the regent for Dharmapāla's son Vanapāla and may also have been the tutor for the young prince as well. The *Nītiśāstra* may have been compiled for Vanapāla's benefit since many of the verses deal with matters of kingship and the proper conduct for a king.

The monastery at Vikramaśīla would have maintained a copy of the *Nītiśāstra* since the Pāla rulers were such strong patrons of the Buddhist faith. From Vikramaśīla there was a steady flow of Indian monks to Tibet who worked on the massive translation project for Buddhist texts from Sanskrit into Tibetan. Each of these monks probably carried a supply of texts to Tibet for the translation project. There is no way of knowing when a manuscript of Masūrākṣa's work was transported to Tibet, but it seems likely that the route it traveled was from the Buddhist center of learning at Vikramaśīla to the translation centers in Tibet. The translation itself was carried out by a Tibetan *lo-tsa-wa* Śakya-blo-gros, who is listed as being a disciple of the great Buddhist scholar from India, Atiśa. Śakya-blo-gros's collaborator on the translation of Masūrākṣa's *Nītiśāstra* into Tibetan was an Indian monk named Dharmaśrībhadra who is known to have done a number of other translations in collaboration with the great Tibetan translator, Rin-chen bzhaṅ-po. The association with Atiśa and Rin-chen bzaṅ-po places the translation around the middle of the eleventh century.

The *Nītiśāstra* of Masūrākṣa is only a small example of the cultural interaction which took place between India and Tibet but it demonstrates the process of such interactions. Tibet assimilated many aspects of Indian culture as a result of the activities of the Buddhist missionaries. Although Chinese Buddhist missionaries were attempting to spread Chinese Buddhism and other aspects of Chinese culture, they were eventually less effective. Since China posed a greater political threat to the Tibetan rulers, these rulers allowed less cultural interaction between Tibet and China than between Tibet and India. The Indian Buddhists who worked in Tibet as missionaries and as translators were transmitters of Indian culture in general as well as bearers of Buddhist doctrines. Their activities had profound effects on Tibetan culture and were important threads in the tapestry of cultural interaction between India and Tibet.

Chart 2.1 : Texts translated by Śakya-blo-gros and Dharmaśrībhadra

Part A. Texts translated by Śakya-blo-gros

Collaborator	Tibetan Title	Sanskrit Title
Dharmaṭrībhadra	Lugs-kyi bstan-bcos	Nītiṭāstra
Dipaṅkaraṭrijñāna	Byaṅ-chub-sems-dpa'i so-sor-thar-pa chos bshi sgrib-pa shes-bya-ba theg-pa chen-po'i mdo	Bodhisattva-prāti-mokṣa-catuṣka-nirhāra nāma-mahāyāna-sūtra
	'phags-pa spyan-ras-gzigs dbaṅ-phyug khar-sa-pa-ṇi sgrub-thabs	Āryāvalokiteṭvara-khasarpaṇa-sādhana
	'phags-pa yi-ge drug-pa'i sgrub-pa'i thabs	Ārya-saḍakṭara-sādhana
	Tiṅ-ñe-'dsin-gyi tshogs-kyi le'u	Samādhi-sambhāra-parivarta
	'jig-rten-las 'das-pa'i yaṅ-lag bdun-pa'i cho-ga	Lokātīta-saptāṅga-vidhi
Śrīṭraddhakaravarman	brGya lṅa-bcu-pa shes-bya-ba'i bstod-pa	Śatapañcaṭatka-nāma-stotra
	brGya lṅa-bcu-pa shes-bya ba'i bstod-pa'i 'grel-pa	Śatapañcaṭatka-nāma-stotra-ṭīka
Janadhana	Ched-du brjod-pa'i tshoms-kyi rnam-par 'grel-pa	Udānavarga-vivaraṇa
Janārdhana	Skyes-pa'i rabs-kyi rgya-cher bshad-pa	Jātaka-māla-ṭīkā
Kumarakalasa	'Phags-pa 'jam-dpal-gyi rtsa-ba'i rgyal	Ārya-mañjuṭrī-mūla-tantra

Collaborator	Tibetan Title	Sanskrit Title
Jñānatṛīgupta	lTuṅ sde lṅa'i dge-ba daṅ mi-dge-ba'i 'bras-bu brtag-pa'i mdo	Pañcāpatti-nikāya-subhāṭubha-phala-parīkṣa-sūtra
gShon-nu bum-pa-can	sGron-ma gsal-ba mdor-bshad-pa'i sa-bcad sñiṅ-gi me-loṅ shes-bya-ba	Pradīpadīpa-tippaṇī-hṛdayādarṭa-nāma
Subhūtiṭānti	mṄon-par rtogs-pa'i rgyan-gyi tshig le'ur byas-pa'i 'grel-pa dag-ldan shes-bya ba	Abhisamayālaṃkāra-karika-vṛtti suddhamati-nāma
Dharmaṭrīvarman	Yan-lag brgyad-pa'i sñiṅ-po shes-bya-ba'i sman-dpyad-kyi bshad-pa	Aṣṭāṅga-hṛdaya-nāma-vāidūryaka-bhāṣya
Part B. Text translated by Dharmaṭrībhadra		
Śakya-blo-gros	Lugs-kyi bstan-bcos	Nītiṭāstra
Rin-chen bzan-po	mṄon-par 'byuṅ-ba'i mdo	Abhiniṣkramaṇa-sūtra
	gCig-las 'phros-pa'i bstod-pa	Ekottarika-stotra
	dPal 'khor-lo sdom-pa'i dka'a-'grel dpa'a-bo'i yid-du-'oṅ-ba shes-bya-ba	Śrī-cakrasaṃvarasya pañjikā ṭuramanojñā-nāma
	bCom-ldan-'das dpal bde mchog 'khor-lo'i dkyil-'khor-gyi cho-ga	Bhagavac-chrī-ckra-ṭambara-maṇḍala-vidhi
	dPal hr-ru-ka'i sgrub-thabs shes-bya-ba	Śrī-heruka-sādhana-nāma

Collaborator	Tibetan Title	Sanskrit Title
	Saṅs-rgyas thams-cad-daṅ mñam-par sbyor-ba'i dka'a a-' grel	Sarvabuddha-samyoga-pañjikā
	rṄal-'byor chen-po'i rgyud dpal gsaṅ-ba 'dus-pa'i bskyed-pa'i rim-pa'i bsgom-pa'i thabs mdo daṅ bsres-pa shes-bya-ba	Śrī-guhyasamāja-mahāyogatantrotpatti-krama-sādhana-sūtra-melāpaka-nāma
	rDo-rje-' chaṅ chen-po'i lam-gyi rim-kpa'i man-ṅag bdud-rtsi gsaṅ-ba	Mahāvajradhara-patha-kramopadeṭāmṛta-guhya
	sByin-sreg-gi cho-ga	Homa-vidhi
	De-kho-na-nīd bsdus-pa'i rgya-cher bsad-pa ko-sa-la'i rgyan	Kosālaṃkāra0tattva-saṃgraha-ṭīkā
	sPyan dbye-ba'i cho-ga	Pratiṣṭhā-vidhi
	bSam-gtan-gyi chos drug rnam-par bshag-pa'i 'grel-pa	Dhyāna-saḍḍharma-vyavasthāna-vṛtti
	'Dod-pa'i yon-tan rnam-pa lṅa'i ñes-dmigs bshad-pa	Pañcavidha-kāmaguṇopā-lambha-nirdeśa
	rNal- 'byor-la 'jug-pa	Yogāvatāra
	gSer-mdog-gi rtogs-pa brjod-pa	Suvarṇavarṇavadāna
	'Dod-pa'i yon-tan lṅa'i ñes-dmigs bshad-pa	Pañcakāma-guṇopā-lambha-nirdeṭa
	rTa'i tshe'i rig-byed sha-li-ho-tras bsdus-pa shes-bya-ba	Śalihotrīyāṭvāyur-veda-saṃhita-nāma
Tshul-khrims yon-tan	Gaṅ-ṭi'i mdo	Gaṇḍī-sutra
	Ma-ga-dha bzaṅ-mo'i rtogs-pa brjod-pa	Sumāgadhā-avadāna

Collaborator	Tibetan Title	Sanskrit Title
	dPe'i phreṅ-ba	Dṛṣṭānta-mālya
Bu-ston	dPal 'khor-lo sdom-pa'i dbaṅ-gi bya-ba'i rim-pa	Śrī-cakrasamvaraseka-kriyā-krama
Rig-pa gshon-nu	dPal bde-mchog 'khor-lo'i sbyin-sreg-gi cho-ga	Śrī-cakraṭambara-homopāyika
	dKyil-'khor spyi'i rim-pa	Sādhārana-maṇḍala-paripāṭi
dPal-gyi lhun-po'i sde	sMon-lam bdun-cu-pa shes-bya-pa'i tshigs-su bcad-pa	Pranidhāna-saptati-nāma-gāthā
Legs-pa'i blo-gros	'phags-pa sā-lu-ljaṅ-pa'i tshig le'ur byas-pa	Ārya-ṭālistambaka-karika
Shes-rab legs-pa	dPal-gyi sde'i rtogs-pa brjod-pa	Śrīsena-avadāna
Bu-ston shabs	Ti-la sogs-pa'i mtha'ki bya-ba'i tshig gsal-ba shes-bya-ba	Ty-ādy-antasya pra-kriyā-pada-rohaṇa-nāma

Chart 3.1 : Possible sources available to *Masūrākṣa*

Masūrākṣa's Verse No.	*Cāṇakya Cr*	*Mahābhārata MBh*	*Pañca-tantra*	*Hito-padeśa*	*Garuḍa Purāṇa*
1.1	587				
2	406				
3					
4					
5					
6					
7					
8					
9					
10					
11					
12					
2.1					
2	582	12.138.24			1.114.15
3					
4	978				1.110.20
5					
6	418	12.138.33	A	B	1.115.45
7.		12.138.25			
8	1076				
9	691				
10	1058				
11	688				
12	355				
13	714				
14	100				
15	220				
	792				
3.1	921	12.138.18	A	B	
2		12.138.52			
3	194	12.138.58	A		1.115.46
4	296		A		1.115.47
5	142	5.37.17	A	B	1.109.1
6	646		A	B	1.115.48
7	890		A	B	1.109.10

Masūrākṣa's Verse No.	*Cāṇakya Cr*	*Mahābhārata MBh*	*Pañca-tantra*	*Hito-padeśa*	*Garuḍa Purāṇa*
8		12.138.17			
9	59				
11					
12	570	5.35.49		B	1.115.52
13	228		A	B	
14	584				1.114.50
15					
16			A		
17					
18					
19					
20					
4.1					
2					
3	15(AB)			B(ab)	1.113.8(ab)
4					
5	15(cd)			B(cd)	1.113.8(cd)
	1009(cd)				
6					
7					
8					
9	566	5.38.9	A		1.114.47
		12.136.138			
10					
11					
12	2077	5.37.53			
13					
14					
15		13.40.4			
16					
17		12.138.27(cd)			
		12.138.27(ab)			
18	801				
19		5.37.28			
20					
21	805	12.314.43			1.112.3
22					

Masūrākṣa's Verse No.	*Cāṇakya Cr*	*Mahābhārata MBh*	*Pañca-tantra*	*Hito-padeśa*	*Garuḍa Purāṇa*
5.1					
2					
3					
4					
5	776				
6					
7					
8					
9	527		A	B	1.109.14
10	6		A		1.114.13
11					
12					
13	83				
14					
15					
16		5.34.62(cd)			
6.1					
2					
3					
4					
5	1422	5.34.32	A		
6	825				
7	844	12.8.19	A	B	1.111.17
8	429		A		1.111.18
9	37				1.109.7
10					
11	1011				1.112.22
12	1-24		A	B	1.110.19
13	964	12.138.37		B	1.114.48
14			A	B	
15	788	12.138.65		B	1.114.49
16	420		A		1.112.17
17	339				1.112.18
18	609				1.112.19
19					
20					
21	474				

Masūrākṣa's Verse No.	*Cāṇakya Cr*	*Mahābhārata MBh*	*Pañca-tantra*	*Hito-padeśa*	*Garuḍa Purāṇa*
22					
23					
24					
25					
7.1	660				11.111.1
2					
3					
4					
5				B	
6					
7	790				
		789			
8	693				1.112.12
9	1023				
10					
11					
12	149				1.112.11
13	162				1.112.6
14	1044				1.112.16
	1045				
15	665				1.112.10
16					1.112.9
17					
18					
19					
20			A	B	

Note : A See Chart 3.3
B See Chart 3.4

Chart 3.2 : Cāṇakya verses

Masūrākṣa's Verse No.	*CV*	*Cv*	*CN*	*CS*	*CL*	*CR*
1.1			a.1			
2	1.3	1.3		1.3		
2.2		.		2.7		7.13
4						3.40
6	5.3					8.42
8	6.14	5.3	64	2.21		
9	6.15	5.4	65	2.22		
10	6.16	5.5	66	2.23		
11	6.17	5.6	70	2.24		
12	6.18	5.7	69	2.25		
13	6.19	5.8	67	2.26		
14	6.20	5.9	68	2.27		
15	6.21	5.10		2.28		
3.1				2.10		5.28
3			38	3.58		8.45
4	17.2					
5	1.6	1.6	27			2.1
6	2.5	2.5	16	3.61		8.49
7	6.11	6.1	31			2.16
9	7.10	6.2				
12						8.53
13						8.71
14	7.12	6.5	7.46			
15	6.21	5.10		2.28		
3.1			2.10			5.28
3			38	3.58		8.45
4	17.2					
5	1.6	1.6	27			2.1
6	2.5	2.516	3.61			8.49
7	6.11	6.1	31			2.16
9	710	6.2				
12						8.53
13						8.71
14	7.12	6.5				7.46
4.3		6.15(ab)				5.39(ab)

Masūrākṣa's Verse No.	*CV*	*Cv*	*CN*	*CS*	*CL*	*CR*
5	2.13(cd)	6.15(cd) 2.16(cd)			1.33	6.15(cd)
4.9				3.47		7.42
18	7.13	6.6				4.15
21	5.2	4.6				5.2
5.5				3.27		
9	1.15	1.16	25	3.48		2.21
10	14.12	5.19		3.94		"S"
13				2.18		
6.6	14.10					
7	7.15	6.8				4.12
8	15.5	6.9				4.14
9						2.13
11						
12			17			3.15
13				1.8		7.44
15				3.40		
16						5.21
17						5.22
18						5.23
21						3.30
22						
7.1		4.7		1.64		4.1
7		4.9	104	1.63		
8		4.8	99	1.52		5.13
9			1.02	1.59		
12		4.11	101	1.57		5.11
13			106	1.60		5.5
14		4.13	103	1.61		
				1.62		
15		4.10	10	1.58		5.10

Chart 3.3 : Verses From Various *Pañcatantra* Versions

Masūrākṣa's Verse No.	*PP*	*PRE*	*PS*	*PT*	*PTK*	*PKB*
2.6	1.170					
3.1	3.213	3.93	3.66	3.94	3.107	
2				3.64	3.75	
3	3.219	3.99	3.69			3.178
4	5.64					5.84
5						1.356
6	1.284					
7			1.26			
13	1.222	1.67	1.59	1.65	1.65	
16	3.35					3.43
4.9	4.12					2.39
5.9	1.52					4.13
6.5	3.58					3.67
7		2.31	2.31		2.52	1.3
8	2.106	2.33			2.54	
12	2.27	2.19	2.19	2.29	2.29	2.32
	4.13					4.14
14	1.428	1.173	1.153	1.169	1.182	1.423
16.						1.248
7.20	1.12	1.9	1.10	1.4	1.7	

Chart 3.4 : Verses From Various *Hitopadeśa* Versions *

Masūrākṣa's Verse No.	*HJ*	*HP*	*HM*	*HH*	*HS*	*HK*
2.6	1.58	4.17		15.6-7		1.57
	4.17					4.17
3.1	4.65	4.65	4.61	109.19-20	4.60	4.66
5	1.43	1.31	1.41	12.15-16	1.36	1.42
6	1.78			18.19-20	1.71	1.78
7	4.1108	4.107	4.104	116.18-19	4.102	4.109
12	3.64	3.59	3.61	84.16-17	3.61	3.61
13	2.127	2.115	2.129	63.5-6	2.122	2.127
4.3	2.9	2.10	2.12	41.13-4	2.9	2.10
	(ab)	(ab)	(ab)	(ab)	(ab)	(ab)
5	2.9	2.10	2.12	41.13-4	2.9	2.10
	(cd)	(cd)	(cd)	(cd)	(cd)	(cd)
5.9	1.18		1.18	9.6-7	1.17	1.19
6.7	1.133	1.95	1.124	25.24-25	1.118	1.127
12	2.146	2.135	2.148	65.11-12	2.140	2.146
13	4.11	4.11	4.10	101.17-18	4.8	4.11
14	2.177	2.161	2.178	70.16-17	2.169	2.176
7.5	1.213	1.159	1.198	36.1-2	1.193	1.200
20	2.39	2.36	2.41	46.7-10	2.39	2.41

* HH verses are listed by the page number and the line numbers on that page.

Chart 3.5 : Post Masūrākṣan Sources

Masūrākṣa's Verse No.	*IS*	*STBh**	*SV*		*SP*	*SRK***	*SS*
1.2	1127						
2.2	3692						
6	2550	266.520	2755	1306			
	4593						
7	4378						AP 35.34
8	7041	262.415					
9	4261	262.416					
10	6950	262.417					
11	5510	262.421					
12	2183	262.420					
13	4427	262.418					
14	694	262.419					
3.1	6013	250.91	2754		266.31		AP 35.36
2	520						AP 113.25
3	1332		2760	1491			AP 35.48
4	1874	268.569					
5	958	260.366					
6	3979	131.1			63.2		
7	5860	250.99					AP 35.85
8	117					469	
9	324					1507	
12	3483	284.945	1344				AP 135.68
13	1506	237.216	2805				
14	3564		2758				
16	5179	2935					AP 65.13
4.1						4662	
3	115 (ab)	248.43 (ab)	2684 (ab)	650 (ab)			DP 7.1 (ab)
4.5	115 (cd)	249.43 (cd)	2684 (cd)	650 (cd)			DP 7.1 (cd)
	6194 (cd)						
9	3433		2734				
12	7217						
17	360 (ab)						
18	5085						
21	5104	286.980			276.26		
5.5	4882	83.59			33.81		

Masūrākṣa's Verse No.	*IS*	*STBh**		*SV*	*SP*	*SRK***	*SS*
9	3214	249.81					
10	64					200	
13	7453					2855	
16	893						
6.5	2984						AP137.9
6	5367	247.7	2759	1428			
7	5409	9.6	2816		52.7		AP137.9
6	5367	247.7	2759	1428			
7	5409	95.6	2816		52.7		AP 100.1
8	2622	93.11		52.15			
9					845		
12	6656	260.362	2757				AP 76.3
13	6293		2756				AP 61.10
14	4069	237.227					
15	4964						
16	2584	234.159		1367			
21	7546						
7.5	5005	233.118			143.3		
7	4976	231.70					
8	6269	238.18		1333			AP 45.4
9	6654	231.76					
12	999	228.20				5156	AP 48.7
13	1089	231.77		1337		5748	
14	6841	229.33					
15	4111	231.78					
20	7322	114.21					

* SRBh verses are listed by page number and the verse number on that page.

** SRK versese are listed by page number and the verse number on that page.

Bibliography

Basham, A. *The Wonder That Was India*. London: Sedgewick and Jackson, 1954.

Bhattacharya, R., ed. *Garudapurānam of Maharsi Vedvyāsa*. Varanasi: Chaukhambha Sanskrit Sasnthan, 1964.

Bhatavadekar, K.S., ed. *Subhāṣitaratnākara*. Bombay: Gopal Narayen and Co., 1888.

Bŏhtlingk, O., ed. *Indische Spüche*. St. Petersberg: Eggers et Co., 1870-73.

Chattopadhyaya, A. *Atiśa and Tibet*. Calcutta: Indian Studies Past and Present, 1967.

Ch'en, K. "The Tibetan Tripitaka." *Harvard Journal of Asiatic Studies*, IX (1946), 53-62.

Das, S.C. *Pag Sam Jon Zang. History of The Rise, Progress, and Downfall of Buddhism in India by Sumpa Khan-po Yese Pal Jor*. Calcutta: Presidency Jail Press, 1908.

Derritt, J.D.M. *Dharmaśāstra and Judicial Literature*. Wiesbaden: Otto Harrassowitz, 1974.

Dimock, E., et al. *The Literature of India*. Chicago: University of Chicago Press, 1978.

Edgerton, F., ed. *The Pañcatantra Reconstructed*. New Haven: American Oriental Society, 1924.

Francis, H.T. and Thomas, E.J., eds. *Jātaka Tales*. Cambridge: Cambridge University Press, 1916.

Ghosh, J. *Bengali Literature*. London: Oxford University Press, 1948.

Hertel, J., ed. *The Pañcatantra*. Cambridge: Harvard University Press, 1912.

Hertel, J., ed. *The Pañcatantra-Tantrākhyāyika*. Cambridge: Harvard University Press, 1915.

Hertel, J., ed. *ṅber das Tantrākhyāyika, die Kaśmīrsche Rezension des Pañcatantra*. Leipzig: B.G. Teubner, 1904.

Hertel, J., ed. *Das südliche Pañcatantra*. Leipzig: B.G. Teubner, 1906.

Hitopadeśa in the Sanskrita Language. London: East India House Library, 1810.

Hoffmann, H. *The Religions of Tibet*. Trans. E. Fitzgerald. New York: The MacMillan Co., 1961.

Hoffmann, H. *Tibet. A Handbook.* Bloomington: Indiana University Press, 1975.

Johnson, F., ed., *The Hitopadeśa*. London: W.H. Allen and Co., 1847.

Kale, M.R., ed. *The Hitopadeśa of Nārāyana*. Bombay: Oriental Publishing Comapny, 1915.

Kale, M.R., ed. *The Nīti and Vāirāgya Śatakas of Bhartṛhari*. Delhi: Motilal Banarsidass, 1971.

Kielhorn, f. and Buhler, G., eds. *Pañcatantra I-V*. Bombay: Government Central Book Depot, 1879-81.

Kieth, A.B. *A History of Sanskrit Literature*. Oxford: Clarendon Press, 1928.

Krishnamoorthy, K., ed. *Sāyana's Subhāṣita-Sudhānidhi*. Dharwar: Karnatak University, 1968.

Lord, A.B. *The Singer of Tales*. New York: Atheneum, 1976.

MacDonell, A. *A History of Sanskrit Literature*. New York: Haskell House Publishers, 1968.

Majumdar, R.c., ED. *The History and Culture of the Indian People*. Bombay: Bharatiya Vidya Bhavan, 1955.

Müller, M., ed. *The First Book of the Hitopadeśa*. London: Longman, Green, Longman, Roberts, and Green, 1864.

Müller, M., ed. *The Second, Third, and Fourth Books of the Hitopadeśa*. London: Longman, Green, Longman, Roberts, and Green, 1865.

Nanjio, B., ed. *The Laṅkāvatāra Sūtra*. Kyoto: Otani University Press, 1923.

Obermiller, E., Trans. *History of Buddhism (Chos-ḥayang) by Bu-ston*, Heidelberg: Otto harrassowitz, 1931.

Paraba, K.P., ed. *Subhāṣita-Ratna-Bhāṇḍāgāra*. Bombay: Nirnaya Press, 1886.

Pathak, S.K. *The Indian Nītiśāstras in Tibet*. Delhi: Motilal Banarsidass, 1974.

Pathak, S.K., ed. The Nītiśāstra of Masūrākṣa." *Vishvabharati Annals*, X (1961), i-52.

Peterson, P., ed. *Hitopadeśa by Nārāyana*. Bombay: Government Central Book Depot, 1887.

Peterson, P., ed. *The Paddhati of Sārṅgadhara*. Bombay: Government Central Book Depot, 1888.

Peterson, P., ed. *The Subhāsitāvali of Vallabhadeva*. Bombay: Education Society's Press, 1886.

Roerich, G., Trans. *The Blue Annals* (2 Vol.). Calcutta: Royal Asiatic Society of Bengal, 1949-53.

Śarma, R., ed. *Saduktikarṇāmṛta of Srīdhardāsa*. Lahore: Motilal Banarsidass, 1933.

Schiefner, A., ed. *Tāranāthae de Doctrinae Buddhicae in India Propagatione*. Petropoli: Eggers et Socii, 1868.

Schlegel, A.G. and Lassen, C., eds. *Hitopadeśas id east Institutio Salutaris*. bonnae ad Rhenum: Eduardum Weber, 1829.

Stein, R.A. *Tibetan Civilization*. Trans. J.E. Driver. Stanford: Stanford University Press, 1972.

Sternbach, L., ed. *The Cānakya-Nīti-Text Tradition*. (2 Vol.). Hoshiarpur: Vishveshvaranand Vedic Research Institute, 1967-70.

Sternbach, L. "The Cāṇakya-Rāja-Nīti-Śāstra and teh Bṛhaspati Saṃhita of the Garuḍa Purāṇa." *Annals of thte Bhandarkar Oriental Research Institute*, 37 (1956).

Sternbach, L., ed. *The Mahāsubhāṣita-Saṃgraha*. (Vol. 1-). Hoshiarpur: Vishveshvaranand Vedic Research Institute, 1974.

Sternbach, L. Rev. of *Nītiśāstra of Masūrākṣa*, by S. Pathak. *Jorunal of the American Oriental Society*, 82 (1962), 407-411.

Sternbach, L. *Subhāṣita, Gnomic and Didactic Literature*. Wiesbaden: Otto Harrassowitz, 1974.

Sukthankar, V.S., ed. *The Mahābhārata Critical Edition*. Poona: Bhandarkar Research Institute, 1933-59.

Suzuki, D., Trans. *The Laṅkāvatāra Sūtra*. London: Routledge and Kegan Paul, Ltd., 1932.

Suzuki, D., ed. *The Tibetan Tripitika. Peking Edition Catalogue and Index*. Tokyo: Suzuki Research Foundation, 1962.

Tucci, G. *The Religions of Tibet*. Trans. G. Samuel, Berkeley: University of California Press, 1980.

Wayman, A., Trans. *Calming the Mind and Discerning the Real*. New York: Columbia University Press, 1978.

Winternitz, M. *A History of Indian Literature*. Vol. I Trans. S. Ketkar Calcutta: University of Calcutta, 1927. Vol III, Pt. 1 Trans. S. Jha. Delhi: Motilal Banarsidass, 1963. Vol III, Pt. 2 Trans. S. Jha. Delhi: Motilal Banarsidass, 1967.

